A New Way to Be Church

Parish Renewal from the Outside In

Jack Jezreel

ORBIS BOOKS
www.orbisbooks.com

ORBIS BOOKS
Maryknoll, New York 10545

Fathers and Brothers
MARYKNOLL

Founded in 1970, Orbis Books endeavors to publish works that enlighten the mind, nourish the spirit, and challenge the conscience. The publishing arm of the Maryknoll Fathers and Brothers, Orbis seeks to explore the global dimensions of the Christian faith and mission, to invite dialogue with diverse cultures and religious traditions, and to serve the cause of reconciliation and peace. The books published reflect the views of their authors and do not represent the official position of the Maryknoll Society. To learn more about Maryknoll and Orbis Books, please visit our website at www.maryknollsociety.org.

Library of Congress Cataloging-in-Publication Data

Names: Jezreel, Jack, author.
Title: A new way to be church : parish renewal from the outside in / Jack Jezreel.
Description: Maryknoll : Orbis Books, 2018. | Includes bibliographical references and index.
Identifiers: LCCN 2018004611 (print) | LCCN 2018014603 (ebook) | ISBN 9781608337569 (ebook) | ISBN 9781626982901 (pbk.)
Subjects: LCSH: Church renewal—Catholic Church. | Parishes. | Lay ministry—Catholic Church.
Classification: LCC BX1746 (ebook) | LCC BX1746 .J49 2018 (print) | DDC 253/.32—dc23
LC record available at https://lccn.loc.gov/2018004611

To Steve and Susan Kute,

whose friendship has inspired me and

whose generous witness heals and brings hope

to the many parts of the world they touch.

Contents

Introduction

This book is about a possible future for the American Catholic Church. In one sense, it is a dream. On the other hand, it is not dreamy, because it simply extrapolates from real, vibrant, and historical expressions of faith as it has been and is being lived by real people and real communities and imagines those expressions in the local church setting.

I am convinced there is a powerful next chapter beckoning the evolution of the parish. It is imbedded in the words of Jesus; it is suggested in many iterations of Christian community throughout the centuries; it is envisioned in the words of Vatican II; and it is proclaimed in the teaching of Pope Francis. The time is here—not just because the current template for parish life is apparently not compelling to most young people and many of their parents, and not just because Pope Francis is encouraging fresh ways to reimagine parish life, but because this paradigm brings us closer to the heart of the gospel, closer to the vision of Jesus, closer to the possibility and power of a transformed life to make the world holy and joyful.

I have spent the last thirty-five years of my life exploring—personally and communally, practically and conceptually, theologically and politically—the linkage between faith and social action. This has taken many forms, from participating as a member of a Catholic Worker community serving in the poorest parts of town, to directing parish social ministry in a wealthy parish, to working collaboratively with some of the largest Catholic and ecumenical faith-based social agencies in the United States, to promoting the vision and practice of social mission in churches all over the country as a speaker and teacher, to creating the JustFaith program. The exploration of faith-unto-compassion has been the primary focus of my work and life.

I have the highest respect for and have invested significantly in religious communities like the Catholic Worker, the Jesuits, the Franciscans, and the Sisters of Charity, as well as national organizations like Catholic Relief Services, Bread for the World, Maryknoll, Catholic Charities USA, and the Catholic Campaign for Human Development, to name only a few. But my true passion has always been how to inspire *parishes* and *local churches* to become beehives of faith-in-action.

Why is that? Because the local parish or church is the place where most Christians celebrate, learn about, and form community around their faith. The local parish is where most people of faith gather to remember their story and break bread. The local church is where most Christians pray to God, form the body of Christ, and become friends. The local parish or church is the default location for people to form relationships and commitments grounded in the vision of the gospel. In short, parishes/churches are where most Christians *are. If the Church is ever going to understand a dynamic communion with God and actualize its full potency as a force for good it will happen only when the parish is at the center of the work of compassion and justice, and the work of compassion and justice is at the center of the parish.*

Throughout the book, there are five critical reference points—personal experiences, really—that inform what is written in the chapters to follow. These begin with a scriptural/theological tradition, first introduced to me as a grad student at the University of Notre Dame (1979–1982), that originally opened my eyes to the necessary flow of faith between reflection and action. This was joined with my introduction to the jewel that is Catholic social teaching, a tradition that had somehow utterly eluded me for the first twenty-four years of my life. With Catholic social teaching came not only *Rerum Novarum* and its later encyclical siblings, but the accompanying theological work of figures like Bryan Hehir, Gustavo Gutiérrez, Walter Burghardt, Jon Sobrino, Walter Brueggemann, John Kavanaugh, and a chorus of others. (Yes, I know, the voices of women were missing!) The voices of these thoughtful men—and the voices of committed and professional women religious I would later encounter in cities and dioceses all over the country—fill this book, both literally and spiritually. It is hard to overstate the importance of good theology that weaves thoughtful reflection on God's presence and purpose with the full embrace of the reality and hopes of the human condition (see chapter 6).

Catholic social teaching, however, is just a signpost for something more important: Catholic social *witness.* Happily, hovering in the atmosphere of Catholic social teaching and good theology is a cloud of witnesses, a gathering of faithful people whose lives make real, as they also embody and inform, both theology and doctrine. Very soon, my education and vocabulary included Dorothy Day, George Higgins, Mother Teresa, Vincent de Paul, Jean Vanier, Jean Donovan, and episcopal leaders like Dom Helder Camara, Oscar Romero, Ken Untener, and Raymond Hunthausen, to name only a very small sample. This robust interplay of exciting, dynamic theology and prophetic, courageous leadership made this period in the life of the US Church both generative and expansive.

The second critical experience that informs what follows was the five years (1983–1988) I spent in a Catholic Worker community (see chapters 4 and 5). The experience of living with and working with men, women, and children, homeless on the streets of Colorado Springs, was the kind of *encuentro* that punctuates the hopes and teaching of Pope Francis. It changed my life. More specifically, it changed my worldview, my self-understanding, my politics, my values, and my faith. That experience insisted, as I became an educator, that faith formation must fiercely proclaim God's love for all with concomitant attention to the well-being and restoration of the most vulnerable. Perhaps more importantly, that experience of kinship with my sisters and brothers living on the street convinced me that it is hard to understand and experience Christian faith without putting ourselves in communion with those on the margins.

Just as important, the Catholic Worker experience was my first taste of living and working with kindred spirits whose common mission was defined by a tireless care for the world. The shared commitments of solidarity with the poor, noncooperation with violence, and living simply birthed a new way of thinking about Christian community that was, to say the least, very different from parish life, the only kind of Christian community I had known to that point. To pray, eat, and work with people passionate about their faith and committed to a love for all people, especially the abandoned, was itself life-giving in ways that I had not previously known.

The third critical experience that informs this book was the eight years (1988–1996) I spent at Church of the Epiphany, a Catholic parish in Louisville, Kentucky (see chapter 9). What began as a tentative, reluctant return to parish work became one of the most extraordinary experiences of my life. Equipped with a formation tool called JustFaith (which I discuss next), a devoted pastor, a diocesan and episcopal commitment to peace and justice, and the unusual opportunity to serve the parish's social mission as a full-time member of the staff, I was provided a very generous workspace for exploring the possibilities of a truly mission-driven parish.

Over the course of the eight years I spent at Epiphany, the work of social mission, which started as the smallest ministry in the parish, grew to become *by far* the largest, fastest-growing, most impactful ministry in the parish. What I learned was that justice *can* roll like a river in a parish. Liturgy *can* reflect and encourage compassion and justice. Preaching *can* speak to social realities of human crisis and suffering. Parish budgets *can* arrange themselves around the needs of the poor. Parish staffing *can* include positions dedicated to the work of social mission. Prayer and spiritual practices *can* engage the world's wounds. Parishes *can* be hotbeds of social action; in fact, when they are at their very best, they can't be otherwise. Parishes *can and should* change the world. There is no need to wonder, debate, or speculate. I saw it happen.

The fourth critical experience was the discovery, if you will, of a tool called JustFaith (see chapter 9). While at the Church of the Epiphany, I crafted an intensive, small group learning process modeled somewhat after the Rite of Christian Initiation for Adults (RCIA) design that focused on linking faith with compassion and justice. It was so profoundly impactful that, in time, it became a national program birthed by Catholic Charities USA and partnered with Catholic Relief Services, the Catholic Campaign for Human Development, Maryknoll, and Bread for the World. It has been used by tens of thousands of people in hundreds of parishes and churches, and with startling results.

Here's the takeaway from the JustFaith story: People are thirsting for the gospel. We all want to know that we are invited to a radical opportunity—a reorientation that liberates and brings life. Our faith can and will ask a lot of us, and we are hungry to be asked. JustFaith not only inspired many thousands of new commitments to charity and justice, not only offered (and offers) an alternative template for Christian formation, but it also provided a fresh and deeper meaning to faith, love, and personhood. We become whole by loving the world.

The fifth and final critical experience is happening right now. As I write these words, Pope Francis is about to finish his fifth year as leader of the Roman Catholic community. I would argue that he has profoundly altered the template of what it means to be pope; he has stretched the expectations of the papacy so that leadership not only includes oversight and teaching authority but *witness.* He is himself a man who obviously walks in the footsteps of Jesus and whose fidelity would be unmistakable whether he was dressed and recognizable in his all-white papal garb or incognito in jeans and a T-shirt; to adapt the popular hymn, "We know he's a Christian by his love." I think all popes to come will forever be measured and inspired by his lifestyle, compassion, lively vocabulary, and fresh reimagining of the Church's commitment to God's world and people.

Pope Francis has made clear that he does not perceive his witness or the witness of any of the great "lovers of the world" whom we call saints to be the private calling of spiritual prodigies. We are *all* called to be people who love the poor, the abandoned, and the wounded. Each of us is called to be a vessel of God's healing presence. Pope Francis has essentially democratized discipleship; we are all called by the same Spirit to the same hope, dream, and reality that inspired St. Francis, Mother Teresa, and St. Vincent de Paul. With that said, each of us is called within a community we call "church." The call must be embraced by each of us, but it is best lived out in community. Pope Francis is not just hoping for "missionary disciples" but a *community* of "missionary disciples." For him, another name for this is "parish" (see chapters 1 and 2).

In addition to recognizing the parish as a place of sacramental celebration, the pope has a dream for the parish as a place of missional preparation, execution, and broad welcome. The parish, in his dream, becomes a place of hospitality, healing, compassion, justice, solidarity, inclusivity, peacemaking, and of course, joy. In many ways, this dream and teaching of Pope Francis—the interweaving of compassion and community—seems like the crescendo and logical conclusion of all Catholic social teaching. It no longer makes sense to describe the social mission of the Church— great love in action—unless it clearly and decisively involves that core of the Church, which is the parish (see chapters 3 and 8).

So, dear reader, if you and your church are ready to put a great love in action, read on. If you are ready for a very new way to be a parish—one that might even inspire and intrigue young people—read on. If you are hungry to be part of a church that asks a lot, inspires a lot, and brings hope, love, and good news to the poor and broken, read on. If you'd like to be part of a church that is exciting, life-giving, and world-changing, read on.

Yes, it's a dream. Of course it's a dream! What life worth living, what faith worth living, what work worth doing does not begin with a dream? Let's dream on together.

1

Vatican I½ Parishes

Most theologians, religion writers, and reporters covering the papacy of Pope Francis rightly identify him as both a product of Vatican II and its principal flag bearer. From the start of his papacy Pope Francis has made this clear with frequent references to the hope and vision of the Second Vatican Council. Equally important, he has made clear his conviction that the work of Vatican II is still incomplete. On April 16, 2013, a month after his election as pope, Francis offered a homily in which he said, "The council was a beautiful work of the Holy Spirit. But after fifty years, have we done everything the Holy Spirit in the council told us to do?"

The answer, he said, is "no."[1]

Pope Francis has reiterated this concern in myriad statements. It is his view, grounded in the best of Catholic theology, that the Holy Spirit is constantly nudging and drawing the Church and the world into a holy evolution, a becoming, that is not yet complete. Vatican II represents part of that evolutionary call. My observation is that, indeed, the hope and vision of Vatican II is yet to be completed, and that this incompleteness has everything to do with the local church's inadequate integration of its fundamental mission.

---

[1] Homily at an early morning Mass in the chapel of his residence, the Domus Sanctae Marthae.

To put this provocatively, most parishes are not Vatican II parishes.

I do not say this by way of condemnation but to make the simple point that there is something still waiting to happen, a spiritually and relationally rich future awaiting fruition. Let me explain.

I do a lot of speaking and traveling each year, and when I am speaking at a parish on a weekend, I attend liturgy at that parish. When I do, I am always very deliberate about picking up a bulletin, because the bulletin is essentially the parish's weekly autobiography. In looking through the bulletin—even quickly—you can usually make a lot of accurate observations.

Occasionally, the front of the bulletin will include a bold heading like: "St. Mary's Catholic Church—a Vatican II parish." When I come across that line I eagerly and excitedly flip the pages of what, in many cases, is a very thick document. But in most cases, after completing my survey, I sadly conclude, "Not a Vatican II parish. This is a Vatican I½ parish!" I mean that literally.

As Pope Francis has suggested, Vatican II was the fruit of an urging from the Holy Spirit for the Church to evolve and grow. Put differently, Pope John XXIII and others at the time were convinced that the Church, which was in danger of becoming stagnant and stale, *needed* to evolve and change. The theology and documents that emerged from Vatican II reflected that change—a change in vision.

To make my point, let me draw from the experience of most Catholics growing up in this country just prior to the Second Vatican Council. The religious or theological education of most Catholic adults in the early 1960s came by way of the most ubiquitous religious education tool used at that time, the *Baltimore Catechism*. From the 1880s to the 1960s, this was the default resource of nearly every Catholic parish for educating young and/or new Catholics. And since there was little else in the way of adult religious education during this same period, most Catholic adults drew from their childhood memory of the *Baltimore Catechism* for understanding their faith and what it meant to be a Catholic.

Here is a sample from the *Baltimore Catechism*, which reflects an assumption that permeates the entire tool. Question #508 asks, "Why Did Christ Found the Church?" In other words, what is the Church's role, purpose, and work? The answer given is, "Christ founded the Church to teach, govern, sanctify, and save all men."

I want to look closely at this three-infinitive phrase, "to teach, govern, and sanctify," because hovering around these words are the assumptions that form the challenge and opportunity facing the twenty-first-century American Catholic parish. Vatican II essentially asks two simple but critical questions about this phrase, "to teach, govern, and sanctify," and comes up with very different answers than the Vatican I Church that preceded it. These two answers, in fact, form the very heart of Vatican II.

This first question that Vatican II asks about the phrase "to teach, govern, and sanctify" is a *who* question. That is, if Christ instituted the Church to "teach, govern, and sanctify," *who* actually teaches, governs, and sanctifies? *Who* are the ministers? *Who* are the active agents of the Church's purpose and work?

Of course, the old answer was "the clergy." Clergy taught, governed, and sanctified. Clergy were the agents of ministry. And, it must be insisted, clergy in so many ways and in so many places have done this generously and well. My life and the lives of millions of people have been enhanced by the pastoral guidance, local leadership, teaching, friendship, witness, and spiritual direction of priests.

However, one of the weaknesses of this answer is that if clergy, who represent less than 1 percent of the community called Catholic, are the only commissioned and active agents of ministry, that means that the other 99 percent—the laity sitting in the pews—are defined essentially as the ones being "ministered *to.*" Again, there is no sin in being ministered to; we all need to be ministered to or cared for, at many points in our lives. But the negative consequence of defining the primary role of the laity as being "ministered to" is that their role is essentially a passive one. Catholics were trained to think of themselves as the ones being tended to, and they assumed—*because this is what they experienced*—that the work of Church, its ministry, was the work of priests, with a generous assist from women religious. So, for example, the language of "lay ministry" was not part of the Vatican I parish lexicon. When the Church addressed the "obligations" of laypeople, as in a "holy day of obligation," the obligation was to show up for Mass, essentially *to be ministered to.*

Now, in stark contrast, the message and vision of Vatican II is that active ministry is not just rooted in ordination, the sacrament of Holy Orders, but in the first and fundamental sacrament of *Baptism.* In other words, in response to the question, "Who is called to be an active agent of the Church's work?" the answer is "Everyone," or all the baptized. A "baptismal faith" means that all who are baptized are called to minister. Everyone is called, not just to Mass but to ministry, to discipleship, to *action.*

And as we consider the transition from Vatican I to Vatican II, we can say that this part of the transition is well on its way. As one piece of evidence, we might refer to the parish bulletin for telltale evidence of the state of the parish; you can find parishes all over the country whose bulletins are filled weekly with descriptions of 146 parish ministries (these are *fat* bulletins). And these 146 ministries are often initiated, led, and populated by the (non-ordained) baptized. If you were to look at the parish bulletins from fifty years ago—typically one sheet of paper—you would find nothing resembling the veritable beehive of activity described in the bulletins of today. It is often the case, as I have observed over the last decade, that when a parish embarks on a building campaign, it is not, as you might guess, to build a new worship space or a school, but to provide more meeting space! There is simply not enough room to accommodate all the groups that have been birthed by the call to ministry.

Clearly, this part of the transition from Vatican I to Vatican II, executed over the last fifty years, has seen great success. To be baptized means that we are *all* called to work, to ministry, and to active faith.

However, not all transitions have gone as well.

The second question that Vatican II posed about the Church's call "to teach, govern, and sanctify" was not "Who?" but "Where?" That is, if active ministry is defined by "teaching, governing, and sanctifying," *where* was this ministry supposed to take place? The answer was that it mostly happened on the parish block.

Let me share a snippet of my young life prior to Vatican II. As a Catholic boy attending Catholic grade school and attending the only Catholic church in town, I remember well the routine of my brothers and sister and I crowding in the back of the family station wagon on a Sunday morning. Past the high school we would go, arguing, laughing, and wrestling, with all the usual rowdy chaos of too many kids in too little space. Past the Dairy Curl we would go, teasing, complaining, joking. Passing the high school, all manner of tumult continued in the back of that car, until . . .

Until the right front tire of the car touched the church parking lot. And, suddenly, because all of us kids were students at St. Cecelia's Catholic School and because all of us were taught by nuns and because all of us knew exactly what we were supposed to do, our voices fell silent, all teasing and tickling stopped, all smiles (mostly) disappeared. And we quietly got out of the car and walked silently and obediently to the doors of the church, and into a building with its oh-so-mysterious stained-glass windows and into a space where a language was spoken that none of us knew (I just assumed Latin was God's native tongue), into a space where smoke from incense would drift up from the altar. Here on the parish block, holy men dressed in black, and holy women wore black habits and distinctive headwear. Here my parents and siblings and I saw and did things we never did anywhere else. We knelt, we prayed, we went to Communion. Only during this one hour on Sundays did we do these things, only during this one hour of stained-glass windows, Latin, chant, incense, kneelers, prayers, priests, and nuns.

Afterward, we would walk quietly back to the car with the same unusual solemnity. But the minute the left front tire left the parking lot and touched the road, it was back to the monkey farm, otherwise known as the backseat of the station wagon. It was back to normal: the warp and woof of neighborhood, friends, sports, school, the beach, and television. And we would live our lives another week in normal time until the next Sunday morning.

And the impression I came away with as a young boy was that this block—as utterly distinctive and unusual as it was—was where the action of faith was located. This was the block where God lived, where church was, where faith was lived out. And, indeed, the faith of my mother and father for most of the years of their lives was a faith that was dedicated to the block called parish property. This "Sanctuary Catholicism" defined a loyal faith in terms that mostly highlighted what was going on at the sanctuary. The logic of Sanctuary Catholicism went thus: the more time you spent at the sanctuary or went to Mass, the holier you were. The more times you went to "confession," the closer you were to God. The more you washed the sanctuary linens, the more meetings you went to on church property, the more time you spent praying in the adoration chapel, the more money you gave to build or to maintain the sanctuary, the more Catholic you were.

This was where the work of ministry happened. "To teach, govern, and sanctify" were activities that took place on church property. As far as I was aware, they did not happen anywhere else; they certainly did not happen in my home or neighborhood. So, church property was where I assumed the work of God mostly happened. As a boy who thought he was going to be a priest, I was pretty sure I knew where I was going to spend most of my time as an adult.

Vatican II, in sharp contrast, insists that ministry is not limited to parish property; ministry is supposed to happen *everywhere.* The vision of Vatican II is that all the world is the geography of God and the place where faith should take us. It is that world—with all its joys, horrors, wonders, wounds, celebration and lamentation—that God is interested in, that Jesus was interested in, and that faith is necessarily interested in. For Christians, this means that the language of "peace" is not limited to the peace we know deep inside after we receive communion and kneel silently in prayer, but also the peace that seeks to end warfare, violence, and hate. The language of "love" is not limited to caring just for our children and friends but requires a broad embrace of everyone, so that we will not tolerate hunger and homelessness, oppression and exploitation, and the dehumanization of widows, orphans, and refugees. And the language of ministry is not limited just to the good and necessary work of ecclesial ministry that occurs primarily on the parish block; the language of ministry is only limited by the time and space of this world. The "reign of God," we learn, has to do with all earthly matters under the sun. So, too, with our faith.

One of the best expressions of this expansive geography of ministry happens near the end of liturgy. There, near the end of the Mass, we hear that most theologically sublime and pastorally powerful word: "Go!" And the meaning is not "Go, because we need to clean up the church now," or "Go, we have prayed long enough."

No, the words are, "Go in peace to love and serve the Lord and one another," or some variation on that theme. It is a part of the Sending Rite, and its meaning is that having broken bread and shared a cup, having once again experienced the presence of the living God, there is but one thing to do and that is to be the presence of Christ in the world, which includes being a vessel of Christ's healing, love, and hope in those places that suffer.

So, for the hour or so that we have been gathered for Eucharist, our touchstones for behavior are the customs, responses, and ritual that are all part of the experience of the Mass. We know when to sit, kneel, and stand; we know the responses; we know how and when to proceed to Communion, and so on. And this shared familiarity and participation are part of what makes for a rich communal prayer experience. Then we are told to "Go," and as we turn our gaze from the altar in the front of the church to the exit doors at the rear and make our way out of the church, we realize that where we are "Go"-ing is back to the station wagon. It's back to the world of family and neighborhood and work. As we gaze out of the church doors to the world around, where we "go" to is a world of political and economic choices, some of which have caused tremendous pain. It's a world that struggles. The world we go to is a world in which over 2 billion members of the human family live in poverty on less than $3.10 a day and almost 800 million people live in extreme poverty on less than $1.90 a day. The world we go to is a world where human trafficking is one of the largest industries and still growing. The world we go to is a world where one in five children in this richest of all nations live in poverty and with food insecurity. The world we go to is a world preoccupied with accumulation, status, and power, all of which are sustained by violence and selfishness.

And as we pass through the exit door to the world outside the church walls, we realize that knowing when to sit, kneel, and stand—all of which serve us well in the sanctuary—is not going to help us figure out how to address, for example, the problem of homelessness in our community or the lack of jobs in rural America or the violence in Syria or the famine in Africa. The touchstones of faith now move from the comforting encouragement of common prayer to the challenging assumptions of faith in action—what we call Catholic social teaching or, even better, Catholic social witness. It is a rich tradition, both life-giving and inspiring.

And here's the problem.

Remember those parishes with 146 ministries in their bulletin? Where do 144 of those ministries meet? On parish property. And what is their focus? The business of the parish property and the people who gather there. And, yes, I am applying a broad brush, but not recklessly. The truth is that most parishes are still pretty much a self-focused reality. This self-focus is not malicious or ill-intentioned, but it's real. One massive piece of evidence of this self-preoccupation is the attention we give, the staff we hire, the budget we create, to prepare our members for sacraments— church block, sanctuary activities—versus the attention we give, the staff we hire, and the budget we provide for preparing people to care for the poor and vulnerable and abandoned. What I observe in my extensive travel for the last twenty-five years is that very few parishes understand that an important part of preparing their members for sacraments *is* to prepare them for the off-parish-property work of compassion, mercy, and justice. As Pope Benedict XVI wrote in *Deus caritas est*, "The Church's deepest nature is expressed in her three-fold responsibility: of proclaiming the word of God, celebrating the sacraments, and exercising the ministry of charity. These duties presuppose each other and *are inseparable*" (emphasis added). Unfortunately, these responsibilities have been separated at the parish for a very long time. This unhappy separation has meant both the obvious undermining of the parish's social mission and the less obvious undermining of its sacramental potency.

In other words, for the time being, you and I live in a kind of limbo between Vatican I and Vatican II. On one hand, we have been called to active ministry as part of our baptism. On the other hand, most of us have not been invited, prepared, educated, trained, or commissioned to do all that baptism beckons us to do, which is to love and heal the world.

So when Pope Francis speaks of Vatican II still needing to be completed, he has this off-campus mission in mind. What Pope Francis is hoping for, I think, is indeed a baptismal faith—*everyone* engaged in ministry, and engaged in this ministry *everywhere.*

The challenge before us is how to expand the geography of being parish. It's time to move from Vatican I½ to Vatican II.

2

A Fresh Blueprint for the Parish

"Completely Mission-Oriented"

In *Evangelii Gaudium*, Pope Francis's Apostolic Exhortation released in November 2013, he makes some remarkable statements about the parish that speak to the paradigm shift from a community focused on the parish block to a community whose focus extends far beyond, with special concern for the wounded places of the world. I have selected five extraordinary excerpts from this document, italicizing a few words for emphasis in each.

First, there is Pope Francis's unambiguous call for change:

> I want to emphasize that what I am trying to express here has a programmatic significance and important consequences. I hope that all communities will devote the necessary effort to advancing along the path of *a pastoral and missionary conversion which cannot leave things as they presently are.* (¶25)

The pope's words suggest that he is interested in something tangibly different happening on the level of the parish, something that has "important consequences." There is something new—a "conversion" even!—that needs to alter the status quo. Indeed, this statement comes from a section of the document titled "The Church's Missionary *Transformation*" (emphasis added).

What is this transformation or conversion the pope is so passionate about?

In this quote and throughout the document, there is an emphasis on the notion of "mission." The words "mission" and "missionary" show up 117 times in the body of the document. One of Francis's favorite phrases for the faithful Christian is "missionary disciple." What is Pope Francis hoping to see happen?

The logic and meaning of "mission" begins, obviously, with the notion of someone going somewhere. Missionaries do not stay put. Driven by the logic of faith, missionaries are sent, and this sending is not random. Like Jesus and the disciples, the driving force of this "sending" is often steered by the compass of compassion. Our steps are steered by the "mind of Christ"; we must go where we are needed, where love is needed, where love has been obstructed. So, as it was for Mother Teresa, Dorothy Day, Damien of Molokai, and St. Vincent de Paul, the "map" for our lives is the Holy Spirit's tug on our hearts to link ourselves with the lives of others who struggle and suffer.

In other words, the geography of mission is not haphazard. It is often motivated by what Catholic social teaching labels "the option for the poor and vulnerable." When love for all—"God's love"—is the motivating force in our lives, we become a people whose lives cannot and will not ignore the needs of our sisters and brothers.

Thus, we leave our home base—our families, our neighborhood, our church, our familiar setting—and, equipped with the nurture and love those relationships have provided, we are prompted by faith to locate ourselves in a new place, a place that might be struggling or abandoned or that we might be inclined to avoid. It should be said, as part of our Christian self-understanding and call, that the love our Christian faith prompts us to go to are the places that the popular culture would choose to ignore. The culture might choose golf courses, the hippest bar, and the beach resort. Our faith takes us to very different places: the poorest neighborhoods, the hospital, war zones, earthquake sites, and sites of suffering and addiction. Our mission is characterized by downward mobility. It is the way followed by many of those we call saints: Mother Teresa, who displaced herself in the streets of Calcutta; Dorothy Day, who displaced herself in the neighborhoods of the poor and homeless of New York City; Clarence Jordan, the white southerner who displaced himself in an interracial community; Damien of Molokai, who displaced himself on an island colony of lepers; and Father Greg Boyle, who displaces himself in the world of urban street gangs. Most holy people spend a big part of their faithful lives with those who have been somehow abandoned or excluded.

So, to summarize, we choose (or we are chosen) to displace ourselves; we relocate. This relocation might be across town for an hour each week or across the ocean for a lifetime, but it's all prompted by the same vision and grace. And the spirit of this relocation, while prompted by the hope of being helpful, does *not* assume that we come with answers, solutions, or plans. Instead, this relocation first seeks relationship. The first step of love, compassion, and mission is not about fixing problems but about inviting relationship. Pope Francis, drawing on his Jesuit background, describes this relationship-driven meeting as *encuentro*, or encounter.

The insight behind the notion of encounter is that relationships can and do change everything. In the encounter with another person we discover friendship, empathy, affection, and care. In the encounter with another person, we also discover their children, their hopes, and their dreams. In the encounter with another person, there comes understanding, connection, and *love*.

So, in this person-to-person communion, we come to affection and new understanding. Conversely, the lack of encounter yields many mistakes and, often, human suffering. For example, while it is popular in some settings to label the poor as "lazy," this distant prognosis suffers from the lack of insight and knowledge that can only come through relationship. During the second term of the Clinton administration, when there was congressional momentum to implement welfare reform, many of the assumptions behind the reform included remarkably ill-informed impressions about the life choices of impoverished people. In a letter to Congress commenting on the proposed legislation, then-president of Catholic Charities USA, Fr. Fred Kammer, SJ, commented, "The welfare reform before you reflects ignorance and prejudice far more than the experience of this nation's poorest working and welfare families." The problem, essentially, was the absence of *encuentro* or relationship. It's just too easy to impugn people whom we don't know. Sadly, we dehumanize both the other and ourselves when we act out of this kind of ignorance. Fr. Kammer's point included the reminder that Catholic Charities was one organization that could speak with conviction and truth about the reality, causes, and cures of poverty. That conviction was rooted in a faithful, longtime accompaniment of those in poverty.

Encuentro, then, is not solely about changing something that is wrong; it is about a communion that changes everyone involved. *Encuentro* changes those who leave home on mission, and it can change those who welcome them. Yes, those of us tugged by love to wounded places might journey in the hope of changing some part of the world, but the experience of faithful people who leave home and family is that we must be prepared to be changed ourselves. The gospel promises *metanoia*, and indeed the mission of encounter and love delivers on that promise. Having formed relationships with brothers and sisters who have experienced hardship and abandonment, we will not remain the same.

One of the great testimonies to this metanoia of the missionary disciple is the legacy of Jesuit Volunteer Corps (JVC). Founded over fifty years ago, JVC invites college graduates to commit one or two years of service in impoverished settings both in the United States and abroad.

A not atypical version of this story goes like this: John, who attended Georgetown University and is the son of wealthy parents and imagines his future as a successful (and wealthy) attorney, decides to take a year off before going to law school, and commits a year of service to JVC. He is assigned a location in a poor neighborhood with three other volunteers, with whom he prays and builds community. His assignment means that he will encounter many people experiencing hardship. And something miraculous happens in that year: John is changed. Call it metanoia, transformation, conversion, or reverse evangelization, the reality is that he is changed. The change is so profound, so life-altering, that John returns from this year of *encuentro* with a refreshed faith and a whole new set of values, values that then steer his course into public service instead of the pursuit of wealth and prestige. This transformation is regularly—and with some sense of humor—referred to in Jesuit circles as being "ruined for life." His imagined and anticipated life of comfort and accomplishment is undone by the beckoning of the gospel. So it so often goes for those who say yes to the call of the Holy Spirit.

The implication for the parish, of course, is that it must become a center of prayer, study, preparation, communion, commissioning, and celebration of missionary discipleship. Pope Francis notes,

> I dream of a "missionary option," that is, *a missionary impulse capable of transforming everything,* so that the Church's customs, ways of doing things, times and schedules, language and structures can be suitably channeled for the evangelization of today's world rather than for her self-preservation. (¶27)

"Transforming everything." Wow! It seems clear that the pope is hoping for nothing short of a revolution in the life of the local parish. This revolution, while it must ultimately be anchored in our hearts, will see expression in practical, concrete matters; after all, what's not included in "everything"? This would suggest a significant and exciting rearrangement of the parish, as the transition from Vatican I (sanctuary focus) gets melded with Vatican II (world focus). Everything from staffing to budget to buildings would be impacted in a dramatic way. One way to imagine and articulate this transformation is to recognize that the church's work is no longer just about what happens on parish property but about what happens off parish property (see chapter 3). Thus, everything in the parish must be reevaluated through its expanded geography and responsibilities.

Notice, too, that Pope Francis contrasts this outward-oriented, love-driven mission with its opposite: self-preservation. This is not the time to circle the wagons, to latch onto some fantasy of the "good ol' days" of the Church and to resist a new chapter, a new adventure in the name of the gospel.

Pope Francis goes on,

> The *renewal of structures* demanded by pastoral conversion can only be understood in this light: as part of an effort to *make them more mission-oriented,* to make ordinary pastoral activity on every level more inclusive and

open, to inspire in pastoral workers **a** *constant desire to go forth* and in this way to elicit a positive response from all those whom Jesus summons to friendship with him. As John Paul II once said to the Bishops of Oceania: "All renewal in the Church must have mission as its goal if it is not to fall prey to a kind of ecclesial introversion." (¶27)

That Francis looks forward to a "renewal of structures" in the parish is significant. Notice that he is not asking the Catholic world to pray in the hope that a few more courageous people will respond to the missionary call of the gospel. I think it is fair to say that the traditional and common understanding of "missionary" in the Catholic world has been that it is a special calling associated with religious communities. Within this understanding is the assumption that it is an elite brand of Christianity, reserved for a few. In clear contrast, Francis is proposing that the parish restructure itself with the assumption that the *entire* community is called to mission. This restructuring assumes all are called to this life of missionary discipleship in the same way that all are called to Eucharist. The hope, then, is not that a few more Mother Teresas will emerge but that entire communities will be formed and prepared for a life of missionary discipleship and transformative encounter. It is hard not to get excited at the thought of how much good and power there would be in such a transition.

Notice, again, in the statement above, that the pope seems concerned about a Church that has become self-preoccupied or given to what he calls "ecclesial introversion." Many US parishes are guilty of this self-preoccupation, not because they are deliberately selfish or mean-spirited but because they are simply not structured for mission, do not exercise the call or vocabulary of mission, and may not even be self-aware of the responsibility for and opportunity of sending people on mission. Faith, in this context, atrophies into puny expressions of private piety and spiritual narcissism.

But the pope is not prepared to give up on the parish structure. He insists,

> The parish is not an outdated institution; precisely because it possesses great flexibility, it can assume quite different contours *depending on the openness and missionary creativity of the pastor and the community*. [I]f it proves capable of self-renewal and constant adaptivity, it continues to be "the Church living in the midst of the homes of her sons and daughters." This presumes that it really is in contact with the homes and the lives of its people, and does not become a useless structure out of touch with people or a self-absorbed cluster made up of a chosen few. (¶28)

Notice these words in the pope's comments: "flexibility," "openness," "creativity," "self-renewal," and "adaptivity." These are words that proclaim the opportunity, the invitation, even the obligation to change! Parishes can change, parishes must change, says the pope. These will not be cosmetic changes or small adjustments to current church-business-as-usual; this renewal in the twenty-first century will require us to "rebuild," much as another Francis (the thirteenth-century saint from Assisi) was asked to rebuild the church in his time.

This could and should be a time when parishes begin to experiment with new ways of integrating missionary discipleship into everything related to the parish. I can imagine bishops or pastors engaging their constituencies in a conversation about an exciting, hopeful, challenging new way to be church and inviting all into a new period of parish renewal and experimentation. It's time for some new wineskins for this new wine of mission and *encuentro*.

Finally, Pope Francis issues this astounding challenge:

> We must admit, though, that the (Vatican II) call to review and renew our parishes has not yet sufficed to bring them nearer to people, to make them environments of living communion and participation, and to make them *completely mission-oriented*. (¶28)

It is hard to imagine a more astounding vision for parish renewal! I would have been glad if he had said *more* mission-oriented, or *mostly* mission-oriented. But what he envisions are parishes that are *completely* mission-oriented. It is wonderfully mind-boggling. This speaks to authentic and comprehensive parish renewal.

In the meantime, over the last decade or two, there have emerged multiple projects and organizations that have tried to address the matter of parish renewal. I have watched parishes and dioceses spend thousands, tens of thousands, and even hundreds of thousands of dollars on these programs. While these endeavors have included some important emphases, they were all doomed to failure. What almost all of them lack is "mission." While they are almost all prompted by the well-documented exodus of many Catholics from their parishes, their focus, typically, is on how to make the parish block more inviting, more exciting, more friendly, more prayerful. None of that is bad. However, these approaches all miss the primary point that the local church's mission is more off parish property than it is on property. There is no room for *encuentro* if the church organizes itself primarily around itself. The power of compassion, healing, justice, mercy, social transformation, and evangelization is underdeveloped or stymied in a community that does not understand itself as commissioned for encounter with those on the margins and for the good of the world.

A parish renewal that is completely mission-oriented is, I believe, the only parish renewal that will compel and excite our young people and attract new members. A parish renewal that is completely mission-oriented will redefine the parish as an enormous power for social and spiritual good, well beyond its boundaries and beyond anything we have yet experienced. A parish renewal that is completely mission-oriented is a parish that will inspire, empower, heal, transform, and provide its members with a spiritual and geographical blueprint for their lives that will change them forever.

Completely mission-oriented. It's a hope of enormous magnitude. It's a dream for a compelling future. And it's completely possible.

3

Gathered and Sent

A Way to Rethink Parish Structure

Pope Francis's exhortation that the local parish become "completely mission-oriented" will, he says, require "a renewal of structures" in the parish that is "capable of transforming everything." In this chapter we explore at least one approach to this exciting renewal.

Let's consider the current state of a typical parish in the United States. If it can be said about Catholic social teaching that it is still a "best-kept secret" in the church, then it can also be said that every facet of Catholic life in most parishes is being short-changed. The vision of God's love and justice and Jesus's proclamation of the reign of God and the life journey of compassion and integrity outlined in Catholic social teaching and the Gospels are central, critical ingredients of our mission, our self-identity, and our vision. To put it succinctly and to summarize Matthew 25:31–46, how can we possibly follow Jesus and *not* find ourselves in the company of our sisters and brothers who are hungry, homeless, and hopeless? How, to use Pope Francis's familiar image, do we not take on "the smell of the sheep"?

To the extent that the people of faith are not interested in justice and not engaged in compassion for the poor and vulnerable is the extent to which the US Catholic parish has yet to become what the gospel invites us to. And this only reveals how the existing ministries therein, including religious education and sacramental preparation, have fallen short, have failed the parish, maybe even distracted it. If our churches are not forming or trying to form real-life saints committed to the poor, prophets committed to justice, and disciples committed to the abandoned and downtrodden, then what *are* they doing?

My observation is that while the social mission of the parish—the local church's commitment to the needs of the poor and vulnerable and suffering—is growing and maturing in some churches, it is still mostly underdeveloped, inadequately supported, and not an integral part of parish life in most places. In other words, parishes with a robust and developed sense of social mission are a very small exception, not the rule.

The role of social mission within the life of a parish can be evaluated in a number of ways, but ultimately it depends on our assumptions and expectations. If, on one hand, we think of social mission—charity, outreach, solidarity, justice, and mercy—as little more than one of the extracurricular activities that pastors, staff, and parishes in general can choose from as an optional side dish to the real meal of parish life, then we might be tempted to admire parish social ministry where it happens and shrug our shoulders where it doesn't. If, on the other hand, the assumption is that a commitment to the poor and vulnerable is a "constitutive"—that is, necessary—part of biblical/Christian/Catholic faith, then it should be assumed that parish life ought to reflect this. And, it might be deduced, this commitment to social mission should be reflected in practical and measurable forms of evidence, such as staffing priorities, parish projects, the language of its prayers, homily attention, bulletin space, the pastor's calendar, and budgeting, just to name a few.

Having spoken at hundreds of US Catholic parishes these last twenty-five years, I can only say that I have met a lot of very fine and even extraordinary people, committed in robust ways to the work of compassion and justice; unfortunately, all too often they pray, worship, and work in parish environments that are uninterested in their work! What I mean—and I *am* using broad brushstrokes here based on what I have seen during my travels (there *are* exceptions)—is that, for example, many pastors—I observe a significant majority—are not very engaged in social mission and do not often, if ever, preach on this theme. Many religious educators and liturgists are commonly and disturbingly uninterested in social mission, and then budgets, bulletins, staffing (or the lack thereof), and so-called mission statements resoundingly demonstrate a lack of interest, if not complete neglect.

In summary, many Catholics who come to a passion for justice and social ministry often do so, not because of their parish, but in spite of it. They are often introduced to social mission because of a relationship with Catholic Relief Services, the St. Vincent de Paul Society, Pax Christi, Jesuit Volunteer Corps, or the Catholic Worker, and then discover later and to their surprise and distress that they have been birthed to a conviction that the parish then does not adequately or energetically support. That is, Catholics who are inspired by their own tradition to sacrifice on behalf of the poor often find themselves in their parish unsupported and even eyed with suspicion. How many more times must I hear the story from some young person who has just returned from a stint with Jesuit Volunteer Corps or Maryknoll Lay Missioners working with the poor talk about how their local parish is not interested in anything they have to share and how alone and abandoned they feel? We invite our young people to a life of faith, and if/when they say yes, we abandon them.

The major challenge is not a lack of theological investment on the part of our tradition or church leadership, or a lack of goodwill in the pews, or fallout from the clergy sex-abuse scandal. Rather, the impediment is a structural one, as Pope Francis is keenly aware, found in the "home" of most Catholics; the problem lies in how the parish defines itself. My observation is that bishops and pastors are as handicapped by the assumptions of this structure as those who work in social ministry. The hopeful part is that this structure can be changed, within the most fundamental logic of what it means to be Catholic, prophetic, saintly, and faithful. Indeed, Pope Francis has stated clearly that the parish structure *must* be changed.

The obstacle, to put it succinctly, is that the assumptions of the place where most Catholics gather to celebrate and express formally their Catholicism—the parish—is currently organized in a way that serves to *prevent* a robust engagement in social mission. The current set of expectations about what constitutes membership at the local parish will forever work against any sincere effort to engage most Catholics in their Church's mission.

But there is an alternative.

As I read the Gospels there is a pattern in Jesus's ministry that I think provides a template for our lives, our work, and our parishes. The narrative of the Gospels follows a pattern that repeats over and over. We take it for granted because it is so repetitious: it's the drama of gathering and sending. Jesus, a teacher, sometimes called "rabbi," does what teachers and rabbis do: he gathers disciples. In the act of gathering, he forms them, he trains them, he challenges them, and he enlightens them. And then he sends them. Jesus, the teacher with a life-changing message of God's good news for the world, gathers followers and then he sends them. Jesus's disciples, then, after Jesus has been crucified and raised, also gather listeners and believers and then they send them. So, at its very best, the Church throughout history has mimicked and embodied this alternation between gathering and sending. The Church gathers. The Church sends.

Let me define the terms: Gathering in the twenty-first-century Church is the work of religious education, Bible study, catechesis, seminary, and spiritual formation. Gathering is the work of liturgy or worship—that is, gathering the people of faith to prayer. It is the stuff of retreats and diocesan-wide conventions. Gathering is the work of nurturing, preparation, celebration, education, and discernment. Most of the time gathering happens geographically, as you would guess, at the home base or the mother ship called parish property: gathering happens at the parish. At its best, "gathering" speaks to the sense of "getting ready," perhaps getting ready for some event like baptism or confirmation but, more generally, getting ready for the larger event called the work and commitments of our faith, the work and commitments of our lives. Gathering is what happens at Sunday liturgy or celebrations like marriages, ordinations, and confirmations. Gathering is the many social occasions to be together—fish fries, potlucks, and parish festivals; we gather to have fun and to be refreshed by the pleasure of each other's company. Gathering is the Lenten retreat or the Advent mission or the revival. Gathering is the RCIA. It's RENEW. It's marriage preparation. It's about nourishing faith, nourishing the community, about remembering our story, sharing in Eucharist, and being prepared for the second part of the drama called . . . *sending.*

Sending is about mission. Sending includes helping resettle refugees in our hometowns and advocating for their well-being. Sending is about serving meals at a soup kitchen and working on ways to end homelessness. Sending is about providing a safe place for battered women, providing care for battle-scarred soldiers, caring for the hurricane-battered in Haiti. Sending is Jesuit Volunteer Corps and St. Vincent de Paul home visits. It is the work of community organizing and peacemaking. It's about making a place in our homes for women with difficult pregnancies. Sending is about feeding the hungry, clothing the naked, and visiting the imprisoned.

The work of the gospel, by definition, is that the transformative love we are called to practice knows no exceptions and finds its way to the wounded places. It is the work outlined and given a vocabulary by Catholic social teaching. The proclamation of the reign of God invites a mission statement for our lives. The touchstones of Catholic social teaching include the common good, the dignity of every human life, and the dignity of creation; it speaks to the support of families, good work, and living-wage jobs, attention especially to the poor and vulnerable, and a bias against violence of all kinds. The proclamation of the reign of God is to embrace the gift of life and the gift of creation that God has given and to relish them, to share them, and to protect them. This sending is a necessary part, a constitutive part of what it means to be in relationship to God. Whenever we tend to the poor, hungry, and naked, we tend to Jesus. To know compassion for God's poor, to act with compassion on behalf of the vulnerable, is to know God. Conversely, where there is no compassion, there is no true knowledge of God. An incomplete faith.

You see, the gospel is a drama of gathering and sending. Gathering *and* sending. It cannot be one or the other. It is necessarily and unavoidably both.

Here lies the structural problem (and why Pope Francis speaks of "structural" reform): parishes, as they are currently and routinely configured, are primarily or sometimes exclusively places of gathering. Period. If you look at the parish bulletin, the parish budget, the parish staff, the pastor's time, it's all about gathering. It is *all* about gathering. It's about gathering for Eucharist, gathering for prayer, gathering for education, gathering for fun, gathering for sacramental preparation (which amounts to gathering in preparation for more gathering). So often, the parish calendar is just one big list of gatherings.

Let me be clear, I am *not* bashing gathering. I have dedicated my life to it. I am a teacher, for goodness sakes; you can't teach without a gathering. Gathering for the nurture of faith is essential. We need a faith community, so we gather. We need to learn and be formed in the likeness of Christ, so we gather. We need to be mentored to holiness, so we gather. We need to pray and learn how to pray, so we gather. We need to break bread and share a cup, so we gather.

However, gathering *disconnected from sending* ultimately mutates into something less than the gospel and something less than what is so very compelling about Jesus and the church he inspired. That parishes are typically structured for gathering and not structured for sending has at least two serious consequences.

First, parishes that emphasize gathering and not sending become static because they have lost their mission. Gathering is for the Church, but the Church is for the world. Parishes that do not structure themselves for mission, outreach, justice, compassion, charity, advocacy, solidarity, and peacemaking are parishes that have been reduced to ineffectual expressions of the gospel. Think about it: What authentic or potent religious tradition is primarily concerned with itself? The critical question for parishes to answer is not just, "What time is Mass?" but "What heroic, healing things does this parish do for the world, and how can I be involved?"

Second, parishes that emphasize gathering and not sending no longer even do gathering well, for we lose a sense of what we are gathering *for*, what we're preparing *for*, what we're praying *for*, what we're learning *for*, what we're being formed *for*. Spiritual formation, for example, in the absence of sending, mutates into some pious version of self-preoccupation. Eucharistic celebration gets turned in on itself; instead of "Go in peace to love and serve the Lord," it's, "Go in peace and make sure you come back next week." Period. It's time that we religious educators and liturgists understand that we can't do our job without a focus on compassion and justice, without an eye toward mission.

Parishes lose members not because they are wrong but because they are not compelling, not heroic, not relevant, not courageous. Our children need and want a Church that is heroic—like Jesus, like St. Francis, like Dorothy Day, like Mother Teresa. Our children want to be challenged to their bones. Our children want to be invited to something that will ask a lot of them. So do the rest of us. We want a Church on mission!

And here is the fabulous news. Wonderfully, the Catholic tradition has an extraordinarily robust tradition of sending, expressed in literally hundreds, if not thousands, of organizations, such as Catholic Relief Services, Catholic Campaign for Human Development, Maryknoll, Pax Christi, Catholic Charities, Jesuit Volunteer Corps, the Franciscans, the St. Vincent de Paul Society, Daughters of Wisdom, Catholic Worker communities, the Benedictines, Homeboy Industries, Missionaries of Charity, and many, many more. The Catholic Church has people, inspired by their faith, working with the poor, the abandoned, the dispossessed, and the discarded in nearly every country in the world. Mother Teresa is one of us. Dorothy Day is one of us. Fr. Damian is one of us. Gustavo Gutiérrez is one of us. Oscar Romero is one of us. Sr. Dorothy Stang is one of us. Fr. Greg Boyle is one of us. If you needed a reason to be proud to be Catholic, just look at the cloud of witnesses. Look at the cloud of agencies, the cloud of care and love and compassion that has been inspired, empowered, and set loose by the Holy Spirit in this world by this Church called Catholic!

But—and here's another way to highlight the structural problem—what I find so interesting is that historically almost every one of these remarkable expressions of sending has been lodged *outside* of the parish. You can't join the Missionaries of Charity in your parish. There is no version of Catholic Charities that operates inside the parish. Indeed, the challenge that almost all these organizations have tried to address over the last decade or two is how to *get into* the parish. A prior and even more pressing question is, how did it happen that social mission ever got *outside* of the parish? In other words, why, when I want to serve the poorest of the poor, do I have to look outside of my parish for a way to do this?

So, the final point I would like to address is where we go from here. Happily, we don't have to invent the answer. All we have to do is to look at our own tradition and perhaps a few relatives.

The testimony of the document *Communities of Salt and Light*, written by the US Catholic bishops in 1994,[1] makes clear that the home parish is or ought to be *the* Catholic social mission structure. The document offers a series of helpful, hopeful recommendations that move the conversation along in a significant way. Encouraged by Pope Francis, I would like to recommend a next step.

I suggest that we Catholics look at the broad horizon of our own tradition and notice what structures, over time, most readily enabled and empowered the Church's commitment to Jesus's ministry to the poor and vulnerable. Let's see where the soil has been made fertile for peacemaking and justice. Let's acknowledge where so many of our saints, prophets, and martyrs have come from. We don't have to look far. The answer—one important answer anyway—is religious communities.

---

[1] See http://www.usccb.org/beliefs-and-teachings/what-we-believe/ catholic-social-teaching/communities-of-salt-and-light-reflections-on-the-social-mission-of-the-parish.cfm.

I think we all would agree that, for decades and centuries, some of the most remarkable witnesses to the work of charity, peacemaking, and justice have been women and men of religious communities. A lot of saints, prophets, and martyrs, not to mention our current pope, have been women and men with letters like OSF, SJ, MM, and SC after their last name. And this is really *no* surprise.

The logic of most religious communities is that they had work to do, that they were called to serve the poor and vulnerable. There were schools to build for poor immigrant children; there were hospitals to build to serve the poor; there were people on the streets of Calcutta who needed love. Nobody joined Maryknoll because the Mass times were convenient; people joined Maryknoll to serve. People joined the Franciscans to serve. In other words, the terms of membership were service. The terms of membership meant you would serve, period. Religious communities have been places where people were gathered well, formed well, because they were gathered for a purpose. In other words, *embedded into membership was the assumption of service.*

The extrapolation I would like to make is suggested by the examples of a couple of churches. For many years in Washington, DC, there has been a church called Church of the Savior, a non-denominational church that was pastored by Gordon and Mary Crosby. I have never been to the church but I have read a lot about it, and here's what I know: If you were to have attended the Sunday worship of that church, you would have been struck by the beauty of the music, the creativity of the liturgy, the enthusiasm of the congregation. And if you had gone again and again and then decided you would like to join the church, you would have been given a registration form that asked for your address, family information, *and* what mission team you would like to join. (A mission team was a subgroup of church members who worked on a specific project related to outreach and justice.) If you were to respond with a note that said something like this, "You know, I really love this church. The worship is beautiful, the music is great, the preaching is fantastic, the people are friendly, but frankly I am really not interested in a mission team or any of that kind of thing, but I am so excited to become a member," you would have been told kindly that, well, if that's the case, you can't join our church. Gathering *and* sending. Neither is optional.

There is a Catholic church in Portland, Oregon, pastored by Holy Cross priests. For a long time it was called the Downtown Chapel and now it is known as St. Andre Bessette. It is located in an area where a large population of homeless people—men, women, and children—live. Many of them sleep every night by the doors of the church. The church is located there on purpose; the church, the pastor, the members want to be there. It is meant to be a place that is inclusive, and it has organized itself around the task of serving the homeless. It is indeed a place where all are welcome, where homeless men and women are welcome—welcome to take baths *and* welcome to pray; where addicts are welcome to get something to eat and to find rehab options *and* welcome to liturgy; where the mentally ill can get counsel, both practical and spiritual. It is a parish defined by a critical social mission lodged verbatim in the gospel. Gathering and sending—obvious, clear, critical, and inspiring. Every year young adults from all over the country commit themselves to working full-time as volunteers at this parish because it gathers and sends. It feeds their faith by gathering *and* by sending. It forms their lives by gathering and sending. It gives them a glimpse of Jesus's life and mission by being both gathered and sent.

My purpose here is not to propose these as viable or even satisfactory options for all parishes, but they are suggestive that it is possible to define membership in a parish by both gathering and sending. So, why not?

Why not a kind of restructuring so that parishes ask everyone—*everyone*—to commit to a social ministry, the way communities like Maryknoll or the Missionaries of Charity ask, or rather, *require* of *every* one of their members? Why not, for example, parishes that divide all their members into teams of twelve (seems like a relevant number) and ask that team of twelve, as a constitutive expression of its membership in the parish, to commit itself to at least one refugee family, or one neglected patient at a nursing home, or one at-risk child who needs tutoring and a little cloud of friends? Why not create a list of advocacy options and invite teams of twelve to make a commitment to Catholic Relief Services or Catholic Charities or St. Vincent de Paul or Respect Life and then that team of twelve becomes the catalyst and organizers of parish activity for that organization? Why not teams of twelve—small faith communities—that pray together, study together, *and* reach out together? Why not organize twelve doctors in the parish into a local version of Doctors Without Borders? Why not a team of twelve sent by the parish to Haiti? Why not a team of twelve to start community gardens, engage low-income neighborhoods, and provide produce for needy families? Why not a team of twelve groomed for community organizing? Why not a team of twelve to work with at-risk moms? Why not a team of twelve plumbers to rehab the houses of low-income and at-risk families; we'll call them the "Holy Plumber Society."

And here is where the rubber of the reimagining and restructuring of the parish hits the road: Why not half of the parish *budget* for gathering and half for sending? This would mean half of the collection would be dedicated to religious education, Bible study, sacramental preparation, liturgy, and fish fries; the other half would go to mission trips, budgets for outreach, membership in social action organizations, and investment in affordable housing, to name only a tiny number of the possibilities.

Why not half of the parish *staff* dedicated to gathering and half dedicated to sending? This would result in half of the staff being committed to religious education, spiritual formation, pastoral care, liturgy, and administration; the other half would be dedicated to overseeing parish projects, immersion experiences, legislative meetings, conflict resolution training, partner relationships, and support for the many ministries committed to addressing the world's wounds.

Why not half of the parish's *buildings* dedicated to gathering, like worship centers and classrooms, and half of the parish's buildings dedicated for sending, like hospitality houses, clinics, low-income housing, and literacy centers?

Why not every bit of half of the parish energy for gathering and every bit of half the parish energy for sending?

Does this sound in any way heretical or unfaithful? Instead, might this be the powerful and lively version of Church that would inspire our children and the world? What does the world look like when every Catholic is connected to another human being who needs a hand, or a home, or hope? I say nothing would draw people to church, draw people to faith, draw *young* people to faith, like a church that was always being sent to do heroic, healing, and sacrificing work, and celebrating that work on Sundays.

So, yes, it's a dream. It seems a long way off. Most things worth living for are. In the meantime, in the time between now and then, here's one thing we can all do *tomorrow.* Gather twelve people who want to be sent and get to work. Why not? Let us live now in anticipation of what we hope for in the future, both within the church and in the world. Organize the twelve of you around the needs of the poor. Work for justice. Work for peace. Invite your pastor to be one of the twelve; he himself must be involved for his leadership to be effective. Inspire the parish. Pray together, laugh together, cry together. Give your lives away together. Change the

Church by your good example, just like a young man named Francis did hundreds of years ago and an old man named Francis is doing again.

A few years ago I received a book that chronicled the difficult lives of children around the world living in places of violence. Inside the book was a picture of a young African girl, probably ten years old, who was wearing a sad smile. Where her arms used to be were healed-over stumps—her arms had been hacked off by some warlord. The God I know, the loving and only God I know, is a God who would gather us—gather us in prayer, gather us in study, gather us in community, gather us for Eucharist. And when we had been formed and made ready, that God would send us, and we would want to be sent. And that God would send us to that little girl. And that God would form us in a way that we would not be satisfied until the world was a place where little girls, little boys, and all people could laugh, grow, be safe, and know love.

4

Missional Relocation and
the Twenty-First-Century Parish

As we consider the renewal of the parish using Pope Francis's notions of missionary disciples and *encuentro*, it is helpful to understand that the deliberate engagement of parishes with social mission and Catholic social teaching is still in its infancy. Most parishes, if they're involved at all, have only been at this for a decade or two, three or four at best. Thirty years is an eye-blink in Church history. Whatever social mission looks like today, if it evolves and matures as it must, it will surely look very different in twenty years, maybe even sooner than that.

In this chapter, we explore how the parish might chart a new way to be a healing force. My intent is to prompt conversation, imagination, and some experimentation around Pope Francis's dream of "a church for the poor."

I start in what might seem like an unlikely place: the anointing at Bethany, which includes perhaps the single most misinterpreted text in the Gospel: "The poor you will always have with you" (Mark 14:7). This one sentence might well be the most notorious scriptural justification for *not* doing anything about poverty.

Many years ago, at my first parish job in Colorado Springs, right out of grad school, I invited a very qualified speaker to address the problem of poverty at a large gathering at our parish, attended by a reporter from the diocesan paper. After what I thought was a compelling presentation and during the question-and-answer period, a naysayer in the audience, a member of our parish, proceeded to dispute the speaker's concern that poverty needed our attention. After suggesting that poor people were lazy and that they had as many opportunities as everyone else, he predictably quipped, "Jesus tells us that 'the poor will always be with us,'" by which he—the naysayer—meant that we need not address poverty because Jesus has told us that there will always be poor people, so it's just what we should expect and tolerate.

The speaker, in response, was then quick to point out the numerous other passages in the Gospels that made clear Jesus's compassion for and commitment to those who suffer being poor. Unfortunately, the damage was done; seeds of doubt were sown. Many of those in attendance left with the idea and perhaps the reassurance that it all seemed to be up for interpretation and opinion; even the Scriptures were apparently unclear. The crescendo of all this was that the newspaper reporter wrote in his column the following week that "a Catholic parishioner reminded the speaker that poverty is a perennial problem with no apparent solution." I would have added, "So, back to your untroubled lives!"

Clearly, this is one of those passages that just hasn't served us well. Most of us who have worked in low-income communities or on issues connected to poverty relate to that text defensively or avoid it altogether because, after all, it only causes us problems. However, I would like to explore this text, not defensively, but eagerly, because this text is actually suggestive of some compelling, provocative, and radical solutions to poverty that might helpfully impact how we think about our work, our lives, and our parishes.

First, let's consider the text. I have given numerous workshops on social mission with a focus on poverty, and it's not uncommon for one of the participants to rather innocently and earnestly make a comment like, "But didn't Jesus say something like 'the poor you will always have with you'?" My first response is to ask the questioner if he or she remembers geographically, where in town, this comment takes place.

There are three versions of this "the poor you will always have with you" text, in the Gospels of Mark, Matthew, and John. Mark's and Matthew's versions are very similar, nearly identical; John's, not surprisingly, is very different. I am going to focus my attention on the Mark/Matthew version. Here it is from Mark 14:3–9:

> When Jesus was in Bethany reclining at table in the house of Simon the leper, a woman entered carrying an alabaster jar of perfume made from expensive aromatic nard. Breaking the jar, she began to pour the perfume on his head. Some were saying to themselves, indignantly, "What is the point of this extravagant waste of perfume? It could have been sold for over three hundred pieces of silver and the money given to the poor." They were infuriated at her. But Jesus said: "Let her alone.
>
> "Why do you criticize her? She has done me a kindness. The poor you will always have with you and you can be generous to them whenever you wish, but you will not always have me. She has done what she could. By perfuming my body, she is anticipating its preparation for burial. I assure you, wherever the good news is proclaimed throughout the world, what she has done will be told in her memory."

This story, as it has been given to us, takes place in the house of a leper. What we know about lepers in Jewish society at the time of Jesus is that fear of the disease meant that those with serious skin diseases were often pushed out of town; this narrative is happening on the margins of the town of Bethany. It is hard to imagine that it was plush; in fact, it was probably miserable—it was hard for lepers to make a living—but that's not a detail we get in the story. The point is that this desperate situation is where the story takes place, and that gives some definition to what follows.

As the story unfolds, a woman enters with an expensive and valuable bottle of aromatic oil, breaks the jar, and pours the oil over Jesus. Those gathered with Jesus (in Matthew's version they are described as "the disciples"), sitting there in the home of a leper on the edge of town where things were in short supply, protest—and reasonably—to their teacher: "What's this about? We could have fed a lot of hungry people who are right outside this house with the money we would have made from the sale of this oil!" Notice that Jesus's followers' and disciples' first inclination was to think of those who were poor. They did not think about their retirement accounts or a fancy dinner or a vacation. They obviously were already beginning to understand that Jesus's message was about good news to the poor, and it has inspired them. But what they don't understand is this apparently needless indulgence of an oil bath.

Of course, what follows is loaded with meaning as the Gospel writer weaves in a kind of forecast of Jesus's death. There is a preview of Jesus's burial with this anointing, so the story is serving several theological purposes. To get to our much-misquoted text, Jesus's response to the disciples, in Matthew's version, is remarkable in its clear and matter-of-fact description: "The poor you will always have with you." Here's the setting: Jesus and his listeners and disciples are at the home of a leper, in a neighborhood of tossed-away people, and Jesus seems to state as an assumption of following him, "Look, you're my disciples and because you're my disciples, you will often be in the company of those who are poor because they are part of God's great care. And you will always and forever have the opportunity to respond to their need, as is clearly your inclination and your call. But this is a special circumstance; whether you like it or not, I will not be here much longer. This woman has done a good thing."

Many commentators on this text are also quick to observe that Jesus's words link with Deuteronomy 15:7–11:

> If among you, one of your brothers should become poor, in any of your towns within your land that the LORD your God is giving you, you shall not harden your heart or shut your hand against your poor brother, but you shall open your hand to him and lend him sufficient for his need, whatever it may be. . . . You shall give to him freely, and your heart shall not be grudging when you give to him, because for this the LORD your God will bless you in all your work and in all that you undertake. *For there will never cease to be poor in the land* [emphasis mine]. Therefore, I command you, "You shall open wide your hand to your brother, to the needy and to the poor, in your land."

So, all this should be enough to disavow anyone who would like to use "the poor you will always have with you" as a way of dismissing our responsibility to come to the aid of those who are poor. But I would like to do more with this text.

In the spirit of Jewish Midrash, let me spend a moment with what could well be a surplus of meaning in the text that has, in fact, repeatedly played itself out in Christian history in a most remarkable way. Jesus says to his disciples, "The poor you will always have with you." It is clear that part of what Jesus meant here, drawing from the precedent in Deuteronomy, is that the undeniable frailty of human reality will always mean that some of us will know periodic times of unforeseen hardship, bad weather and poor crops, scarcity, oppressive politics, or exploitative economies, and that God requires of us that we respond to each other's need, in first-person care. This simply acknowledges that human life in this world is vulnerable and that God has given us to each other to protect each other from the vicissitudes of human life and adversity.

As good as that is, I think it gets better.

Now let me repeat this English version of the text with added and focused emphasis: "The poor you will always have *with you.*" Is it possible, sitting in the home of a leper, that what Jesus also meant here is that his disciples were to understand their place, their *default location,* is *with* those who are in harm's way? That is, those who would follow Jesus will not just care, as needed, for the poor who somehow come into their lives but will necessarily and deliberately seek out and locate themselves in the places where life is just hard, to share in the life of the community, to speak a word of hope, to be helpful, and to help rebuild a community of shared love and resources.

Does the text suggest something along the lines of what we might call holy displacement or Spirit-led relocation? I am thinking here—probably because I can't escape my Catholic Worker past—of Dorothy Day. But I am also thinking of Fr. Greg Boyle. And Mother Teresa. And Damien of Molokai. And Jean Vanier. Is there a basic Christian instruction here? Is Jesus saying, "To be my disciple, you will locate yourself where those who struggle are"? Notice that I am using the word "locate," so as to be a little ambiguous. But in the case of Dorothy Day, Greg Boyle, Mother Teresa, Damien of Molokai, and Jean Vanier, it is not ambiguous: they physically relocated, as in *made their residence with*—the way Jesus *dwelt* among us.

Our faith tradition seems to inspire in those of us who are not poor a reckoning with the possibility of Spirit-driven relocation. I mean, to be perfectly clear, that our faith tradition, our Scripture tradition, our moral tradition, and the witness of holy people all suggest the possibility that we make our homes, make our livings, make or remake our lives—make time—in the neighborhoods where our sisters and brothers who are poor and vulnerable are. The annals of Christian history include a long list of people who have made such a choice to relocate themselves to vulnerable places, war-torn places, poverty-stricken places. (The flip side is that we are simultaneously encouraged to avoid locating ourselves in the places that are out of sight of those who struggle; see the parable of the Rich Man and Lazarus in Luke's Gospel.)

Any list of saints includes an inordinate number of people who chose unlikely mailing addresses and lived their lives in the communities of those who see life from the bottom up. How many of us have at least pondered the prospect that maybe we should work and live in, well, Haiti? We know this tug, if only occasionally, don't we? Moreover, we celebrate the lives of people like Dorothy Day, Greg Boyle, and Jean Donovan (the lay missioner who was killed in El Salvador) not as kooks or extremists but as holy heroines and heroes. Unhappily, in our parishes we think of this kind of relocation and ministry as a kind of peculiar calling—dramatic, extraordinary, and admirable but just for a special few. It's not part of what we would dare expect of one another, not an option on the parish registration/participation form. We might hope of each other that we write letters to our government officials in the name of childhood poverty, but we would not even think it plausible that one of us might move to the poor side of town as a matter of faith.

Might we, could we, mustn't we take this possibility of displacement and relocation more seriously, as a matter of fidelity, as a matter of impact and strategy, and *as a matter of parish life*?

The language of solidarity in the Catholic tradition is an intricate, lovely, and potent concept. Jeffry Odell Korgen has written a book about Catholic Relief Services titled *Solidarity Will Transform the World*. I believe that. Solidarity speaks to the unity of creation—all is of God, all is one, all is connected. Solidarity speaks to a spirituality that understands that every human being is my sister or brother. Solidarity gives moral logic to the importance of addressing injustice. At the heart of the gospel, it's all about recognizing each other as kin and precious, responding to each other with open hands and wide hearts, and recognizing God's very self in the warp and woof of compassion and care. The closer we get to and are focused on relationships, the better off we are. Community and solidarity are spiritual siblings.

Moreover, it is hard to imagine a more potent version of community and solidarity than being a part of each other's life in the same neighborhood, sharing joys and struggles. Relocation turns the spiritual, scriptural, imagined "neighbor" into a real-life neighbor. In the legacy and witness of the Church, I am struck by how significant it is and how transformative it has been for people to choose to make a preferential option for the poor with their physical presence. The intentional migration of people, individually and sometimes communally, from comfortable places to places of crisis constitutes some of the most critical witnesses we have as a religious tradition. As I mentioned before, these stories abound in the lives of the saints; this is an important part of the Church's witness.

Consider the work of Maryknoll, for example. I am just amazed and delighted that some young man from the Baltimore suburbs would join the Maryknoll Fathers and Brothers, or some young woman from Omaha would join the Maryknoll Sisters, be asked to go to a poor village in Tanzania, never question the assignment, spend forty years there, and, when asked, only talk about how much he or she loves it. But, for whatever reason, you won't find the option of relocation in the parish social ministry to-do list. You might be asked to work at the soup kitchen or write a letter to your congressperson or donate to a worthy cause, but it is just about guaranteed that the parish is *not* offering the opportunity to move from our comfortable home to Tanzania or even to a poor neighborhood on the other side of town.

Is it time for us to look seriously at this undeniable gift of the Holy Spirit—this tug to put our bodies where our hearts want to go—as we continue to dream the possibilities and potency of parish renewal?

Now before you check out on me in protest, hang on. You might be one of those who is already very committed and right now you're thinking, *Look, I have given my life to this work. I spend my free time in legislators' offices, I fundraise for Catholic Charities, I receive thirty-six emails a day from some social justice group, I work at the local soup kitchen, and all I have to show for it is a dumpy car and an occasional pat on the back. And now you want me to move from my comfortable home to the tough side of town or to Haiti?*

Fair enough. So let me recast this conversation so that it doesn't feel like a burden. I am not trying to make our lives harder.

Let me offer this playful but earnest observation. We use many words for Jesus: teacher, rabbi, savior, redeemer, prophet, Son of God, and messiah. I embrace all of those, but I have one I'd like to add for your consideration: life coach. I would suggest that the language of guru, teacher, sage, prophet, spiritual master, and rabbi fill a function that today also gets popularly described as life coach. And while I am not a hip kind of guy (I don't even do Facebook), and I am not much into contemporary fads and fashions, and *I* don't have a life coach, except the one named Maggie (my wife), I think the language of life coach is a helpful description.

What I like about Jesus as "life coach" is that it puts a dual focus on the *relationship and the practice*—between the coach and the coached (and the consequences). It's interactive and inseparable. If I only call Jesus "Redeemer," then it can too easily translate into a passive relationship: Jesus has saved the world, saved me, thanks be to God. I can stand at a safe distance. But if I call you "coach," and even "life coach," then I have a relationship to you as the coached and it has to do with how I respond to your coaching. This just seems to me to be a lot more interesting and maybe even more accurate, when it comes to our interaction with the Jesus of the Scriptures.

To try to soften some of the prickly edges of religion as an unyielding belief system as well as the presumption of the tragic consequences for those who get it wrong, what if we think of Jesus as a life coach who is providing stories, challenges, exercises, and pilgrimages to help us *explore* life and love, and to discover and *experience* God, instead of just having opinions about God? The focus becomes not rigid orthodoxy (right belief) but rather orthopraxy (right practice), or even better, as Gandhi would say, living experiments with truth, or even experiments with love and faith.

Here's my main point: The way to think about Jesus's teaching, I am suggesting, is *not*, "Do this or go to hell," but rather, "Here is an exercise for your life, for you to try; see what happens. It could be pretty great. If not, we'll try something else." Experiments in discipleship. I am not trying to be goofy or heretical. I just want us to think about this social mission business with a lighter heart and an openness to try some adventures that we might otherwise dismiss too quickly. Our time is too short for our faith and life to get stuck in a rut. What's more, as Pope Francis reminds us, we don't need "sourpusses."

It seems that, for those of us who take Jesus earnestly and who are not poor, there can be a spiritual/moral tug to relocate. So, let's first acknowledge it; then let's explore it and experiment with it as a kind of spiritual exercise.

One of the Catholic traditions that experiments with this tug is the Catholic Worker movement. Dorothy Day and Peter Maurin interpreted the call of Jesus as an invitation that the Church, the followers of Jesus, needed to be in the places where Jesus was particularly attentive in his life. I was a member of a Catholic Worker community for five years, and its significance continues to intrigue me. I think it's a model that is worth our consideration as we think about a new template, a new structure for parish life.

By way of autobiography, I'd like to share a small piece of my personal experience with a Catholic Worker community and its work and effects. Some experiences in our lives seem to exert an impact that is somehow definitive, and this was one of those for me. I should mention that when I joined the community I was young, naive, and clumsy; all I did was try to fit in with the already well-established life and structures that were solidly in place.

After I finished my master's degree at Notre Dame, I moved to Colorado Springs to take a job at a parish working in adult formation. After only a couple of weeks, I started to hear about this group of people who were living and working together, using the Catholic Worker model. This introduction climaxed with an invitation, a few weeks later, by one of the leaders of the community, a man named Steve, to "have dinner" together. Dinner, as it turned out (and to my surprise), took place at one of the hospitality houses where I sat down with ten formerly homeless men and women; we were all served by our host, Steve, who sat down last after everyone had been served. For this rather protected, insulated young man, it was blowing all my theological circuits. I thought to myself, "This just looks too much like the Gospel" (think Luke 14:13).

I was twenty-five years old. I had studied theology for seven years. I was a very serious Catholic. This experience was exactly what I needed and, without knowing it, what I was looking for. Parish life wasn't doing it for me, because at age twenty-five—

passionate, energetic, and zealous—the parish's rather domesticated focus on Bible studies, bingo, fish fries, and potlucks was not calling my name.

I asked to join the community and they welcomed me. I quit my parish job, sold my house, sold my car, and spent the next five years supervising our soup kitchen; staffing one of the hospitality houses that was home for men and women, most of whom suffered from mental illness of one kind or another; advocating for the poorest people in our community; sharing our experience with churches all over the city; and making a lot of people's lives much more livable than they otherwise would have been. Oh, the dozens, if not hundreds, of painful stories that my wife, Maggie, and I could tell about our friends who were once living in cardboard boxes or abandoned vehicles or boarded-up shacks, tortured by addiction, illness, and/or fear, but who, because of this Catholic Worker community of fifteen adults and their children, made their way to a community and a home where there was good food, security, and support. This was a community where everyone's birthday and holidays and simple victories were celebrated with gusto, where there was friendship and care. Much good was done. And one of the great graces of my life was that I got to be a part of it.

We lived with those who were homeless, we ate with those who were poor, we celebrated with those who were ill or disabled. We never used the language of "ministering to the poor," which creates awkward distinctions and separations. We were just doing what we thought life, faith, and God would expect of human beings: being hospitable, welcoming, and helpful to each other. The Catholic Worker ethos assumed that this was a normal and faithful way to live life; it was not understood as exercising a special function. This was not a hobby, a break from "normal life," or disconnected from the rest of life. It was just the life of faith in action.

Happily and necessarily, this was done in community. Church is a collective exercise. We follow Jesus in a pack, or we probably don't follow Jesus at all. The Catholic Worker response to the poor and homeless was unimaginable without the presumption of a community doing it together. This was the context in which we were able to address some of the world's pain *and* I was able to develop some of my most intense friendships, including the one with my wife-to-be. Doing important things with each other is one of the quickest routes to affection and friendship. To work and live together was also an awful lot of fun.

At the same time, this life asked a lot of me. I so very much wanted that. I wanted to be changed. I wanted to do something important. I wanted the opportunity to make sacrifices. I wanted to see what it felt like to walk in the tradition of those whom we called saints. I wanted to experience that life. I learned to like myself a lot more when I realized that my life could impact someone else's so significantly. It allowed me to give myself away and, in doing so, ironically, rediscover my life.

I loved living and breathing the air of faith twenty-four hours a day. This was a Christian community, a Christian lifestyle, a Christian way of being, a Christian response to human suffering. We tried to integrate into every decision the logic of the gospel, Catholic social teaching, and a preferential option for those who were poor and most vulnerable. We lived with very little. We tried to live nonviolently. We took prayer seriously. It was a great way to be formed as a young man.

What, then, might the Catholic Worker tradition offer to us as we consider the future of the American Catholic parish?

First, the Catholic Worker movement, like L'Arche, like Maryknoll, like Greg Boyle and Homeboy/Homegirl Industries, like so many religious communities, is a response to a constant pulsing and prompting of the heart, of the Spirit, of God, of grace.

The prompt to be with those who are vulnerable is the same prompt that draws us to a lost and crying child. We are made in the image of God, who is linked with us so deeply that, like the parent of a sobbing child, God is especially present to the little ones who weep. So, too, when our eyes are open and our hearts are large and our arms are wide, we are inclined in the direction of being present to those who have been left behind.

Those of us who have been formed and groomed by the twenty-first-century American assumptions of upward mobility, accumulation of wealth, and unquestioned consumerism *need* an opportunity to hear a voice inside that may be speaking softly amid the noise of all that distraction. We need someone to tell us it's okay, even good, to listen to that voice, that there are other options besides seeking wealth. In the name of love, yes, it's normal to be tugged by the lives of those who are poor. Yes, it's okay, even important, to be tugged by what's happening on the difficult side of town. It's important to visit Haiti; in fact, it's even okay to move to Haiti. It's okay to move to a poorer neighborhood. In fact, it's great. Some of us will do relocation in our free time, with St. Vincent de Paul home visits; some of us will do this on our vacation time with mission trips; and some of us, maybe more than we think, will want to do this full-time, *if but given the chance.*

Specifically, our parishes and dioceses could be, should be, places where people are given the opportunity, the call, and the support to make a choice to relocate spare-time, part-time, vacation time, or full-time with those who are in harm's way. To emphasize the last option, parishes, like religious communities, like the Catholic Worker, should presume and plan to invite *some* of its members to choices that allow full-time relocation. And I would argue that the parish should be the catalyst, the funder, and the support for such choices.

Rather than assume that people with a felt need to make a commitment to relocate must search out some other agency, the parish must become a place that includes the opportunity to do big things. Let me emphasize that I am not presuming that everyone fits into this category, but a lot of people are able and are looking for a new life challenge. Their interests and energies have not been accounted for in most parish planning, it seems to me. As a case in point, I am all too aware that people who have done the Peace Corps or Jesuit Volunteer Corps or Maryknoll Lay Missioners return home after those experiences and look for ways to express their life energies in the local faith community. Frequently, they feel like strangers in a strange land, surrounded by fish fries, bingo, and basketball leagues. They frequently leave parishes quietly, not because they don't want to be Catholic, but because they can't find a way to be faithful there to the God they have known. The point is that the parish as the Catholic beehive should offer a variety of options to parishioners, including some that allow for a big commitment like relocation with those who struggle.

Most parishes present a dynamic we might call "the tyranny of small expectations." It gets played out like this: a volunteer or staff member comes up with a big idea and shares it with the leadership team. Almost immediately, someone says, "You know our people are busy. If we're going to offer something, it has to be short, quick, convenient, and easy." Unfortunately, what you get when you offer something that is short, quick, convenient, and easy is almost nothing. My experience is that lots of people are wandering around church property not looking for the *smallest* thing to be asked of them. Short, quick, convenient, easy churches end up losing their members, probably due to boredom. I think this reality names the crisis that many churches face today with the loss of their young people.

Here's the thing about gospel relocation. It probably won't happen if we're not invited. It won't happen if there's no opportunity. Unless someone says, "Have you considered moving a part or all of your life into a different neighborhood?" most of us will not consider it. In other words, relocation must be part of the vocabulary of our parish home. And it must get structured—like a Catholic Worker community, like Jesuit Volunteer Corps, or the Missionaries of Charity, or any of the versions of the new monasticism that are popping up in cities around the country. It must not be thought of as a heroic choice, just a standard part of the lexicon of Christian commitment. If, indeed, we think of it now as an extraordinary commitment, it is only because it goes unspoken, unmentioned, even unimagined. Conversely, give kids a chance to spend a year or two living and working in at-risk communities after they graduate from college, and guess what? They'll do it. Last year, one out of ten of the University of Notre Dame's graduating seniors took that option. But if you don't offer it, if you treat it like an unlikely possibility, you will only get what you expect: nothing.

To paint a picture of how a parish might effectively implement a strategy of holy displacement, I propose that parishes sponsor a Catholic Worker–style hospitality house in a neighborhood where homeless and low-income men and women and families are. To get practical, this could mean, first, studying the Catholic Worker tradition and then inviting someone from a nearby Catholic Worker community to share their experience. From there it could involve purchasing an abandoned structure, engaging the parish in the rehab, and inviting the parish to join in the fundraising for the expenses of purchase and renovation. From there the work would include organizing teams of people to cook, to staff, to offer medical support, to assist with work or educational opportunities, to offer after-school activities for children, or just to be present at the house and in the neighborhood for welcome, conversation, and friendship.

Such a project could and would engage lots of people in the parish who would have the opportunity to form personal relationships with those who, for example, experience homelessness, joblessness, and poverty. Real community would be the primary aim. Food stamps is not the crescendo response to poverty; community is. What we all desire is not just food but sharing a meal with people we care about and who care about us. That is true for my kids, and it is true for those who roam the streets without a roof. Building community is something we can and must do if we're serious about healing the world's wounds.

With more Christian churches than post offices, we have the capacity to provide an enormous welcome, and a lot of friendship, in addition to food and shelter. An ongoing, sensitive, living presence in a neighborhood that's been left behind might well be a most transformative possibility for both the neighborhood and the church. Some members of the parish may want to participate monthly, or weekly, or on the weekends; some members of the parish might choose to commit themselves full-time as volunteers or even residents. For every Catholic Worker community that I know of, with only a handful of full-time members, there are one hundred, maybe one thousand part-time volunteers. Commitments like this are leaven for a wider community commitment, and a little leaven makes for a lot of bread. A few relocated people can make for a very large and active beehive.

Then what happens? The neighborhood just might change. There will be people who find their voice, find the right medication, find a job, find some new friends, maybe even find a new faith. There will be some who will get to go to school, who get a chance to hope, who get a new start. New skills will be learned, new jobs will be created, new imagination will be inspired. Drug use will diminish, guns will go silent, empty buildings will fill. Children will walk in safety and even flourish. I have seen all this happen.

And the people in the parish will change. For many it will set in motion a new life orientation. These people, inspired by their experience, will become advocates who will find their way to Catholic Charities and Catholic Relief Services and Catholic Campaign for Human Development and St. Vincent de Paul. There will be those who start Pax Christi groups, speak to your JustFaith groups, and get involved in forming our youth. There will be those who will run for political office, start businesses, and have children. There will be those who give money, show up for lobby days, and vote. There will be those who become priests and nuns, who will lead nonprofits, who will become catechists and liturgists. There will be those whose lives will be forever changed by walking hand in hand with those who had been pushed away; it will be—as it has always been—holy ground, and life will never be the same. I have seen all this happen.

The poor *we will have with us*. And they *will have us with them*. And because of bread and love, the poor will no longer be poor. And we will all be richer than we have ever been.

I think Dorothy Day and Jesus had that in mind.

5

Marriage with a Mission

A Sacramental Love Story

Pope Francis's encouragement that the Catholic parish become "completely mission-oriented" invites a comprehensive reimagining of all of parish life. Just what would it mean for all parish activities to "completely" integrate a mission orientation? For example, how would religious education be impacted? How would the liturgy change? What staff positions would be created or recommended by this reimagining? Would the baptismal rite be altered? How would the role of the pastor be redefined? Would parishes start creating nonprofit ministries to address critical needs in the community? It's exciting to think about.

As I have imagined and engaged the possibilities for parish renewal over the years, I have often considered how a mission orientation would impact the way we think about and prepare people for marriage. To be forthcoming about my interest, I have often reflected on how grace-filled and satisfying my marriage with Maggie has been, which was birthed, in large part, by a shared interest in mission, compassion, and justice.

Maggie and I first met while I was a member of a Catholic Worker community. Shortly after that, Maggie joined the community, and the beginning and early chapters of our relationship were framed by the work and vision of the Catholic Worker experience. The community of 15 we were a part of oversaw the operation of a soup kitchen that served lunch each day to 250 to 350 people. We also ran and staffed three hospitality houses for men and women who were suffering homelessness. A great many of our guests at the soup kitchen and hospitality houses struggled with mental illness or addiction, sometimes both. Our guests often included children.

The community was also committed to peacemaking, and it was not uncommon for one or more members to be in jail for having committed an act of nonviolent resistance in response to political decisions that promoted violence or unnecessary military engagement. Maggie and I, believe it or not, got engaged while she was in jail for having occupied a legislator's office in protest of his vote to fund a terrorist group in Central America. I figured that proposing to her while she was incarcerated might be good timing, since her prospects at that moment were fairly limited.

We tried to live simply. Most of us rode bikes to get around; three cars were shared by the fifteen adults. We lived in modest housing. Some of us lived full-time with formerly homeless guests; most of us shared low-rent or no-rent dwellings in distressed neighborhoods. While none of us had full-time paid jobs so that we could focus on the projects and efforts of the community, the pay we received for our labor at part-time jobs was shared in common to pay all bills. After bills were paid, each of us received a crisp, clean five-dollar bill each week for recreation, although it needs to be said that some members shared their five-dollar windfall with our friends on the street.

We chose not to have health insurance as a sign of solidarity with the poorest people in the community and as a way of honoring Jesus's encouragement that we "not worry about tomorrow;

today has enough worries." To put it slightly differently, we were interested in spending our resources on the profound need we saw around us today rather than the needs we might or might not have tomorrow.

Most of us had few clothes, and that which we had was typically well worn. We took few, if any, vacations. We owned very little.

Doesn't sound too romantic, does it?

In fact, it was great. This, as it turned out, was an extraordinary way to begin and to frame the expectations and hopes and dreams of marriage. Here are six brief reflections on why I think this "missional orientation" has made for a rich and life-giving relationship between Maggie and me and why it might be important for others.

1. Maggie and I met, courted, and married with a shared assumption that we would spend the rest of our lives together working to address the needs of those impoverished, living simply, acting nonviolently, and exploring our faith with an ardent intentionality. We could not imagine ourselves taking jobs just to get wealthy or living in an affluent neighborhood or maxing out a credit card. In other words, there was a binding vision of what our lives would look like. It was a narrative that we have since spent our lives trying to live into, often inadequately. However, this shared vision or narrative provided a set of touchstones that would serve to anchor our choices, inform our shared lifestyle, and correct our missteps. Over the years, Maggie and I have relied, in varied and changing ways, on the reference points of prayer, compassion, simplicity, and community as the primary signposts by which to live our lives with a sense of integrity and fidelity.

While Maggie and I chose to leave the Catholic Worker community shortly before the birth of our second daughter, the lived experience of caring for those who were homeless, having few things, and working and living with other people in community were so profoundly life-giving that they have guided our steps through the many chapters of our lives since then. For example, when I decided later to work at a parish, the job I sought was a position focused on outreach and justice. Later, when Maggie and I decided to farm full-time, we opted to explore the possibilities of simplicity, building a straw-bale house without running water, electricity, or telephone (with three young daughters!). When an invitation came our way to start an organic farm project at the Sisters of Loretto Motherhouse in Central Kentucky, we rejoiced that we would be surrounded by a Christian community of so many fine and committed women.

In short, the shared embrace of the gospel vision of a world made holy only by generosity, care, and mutuality has guided and enriched our shared life together.

2. There is a powerful but little-discussed linkage between compassion and passion. Yes, loving Maggie was/is not all about solving the world's many problems. I love her. And when I was a young man, I fell in love with her and loved her like any self-respecting young man would love his young and alluring spouse. Little has changed in that regard. However, as any experienced married person reading these words knows, passion and being in love come and go. One of the great and underrated falling-in-love and being-in-love experiences is to witness your partner's generosity and care for others. I am very aware how much I can fall back in love each time Maggie does yet another generous, patient, and sacrificing deed for someone else. Sometimes that "someone else" is a family member, but just as often it is someone on the street, in prison, or just in pain.

I have a memory of when Maggie and I were living on a farm; money was always tight. When our youngest child was old enough to attend school, Maggie decided she would go back to work to help with finances. As someone who had always dabbled in art, she was planning to apply for a part-time art teacher position that had opened at a local school in rural Kentucky where we were then living. She was excited about it because she loved art and thought she would enjoy teaching art to kids. She went off that morning to interview at the school.

When she got back home I asked her how it went. She told me that she got *a* job, but the way she said it made me curious. "Did you get the art teacher job?" I asked. "Well, yes," she said, "but I decided not to take it." And then I listened as she shared what had happened. The school had need for someone to work one-on-one with a little boy with a rare and devastating disease called Lesch-Nyhan Syndrome that results in a neurological condition that interrupts motor skills and, strangely, triggers children to hurt themselves. The condition looks like cerebral palsy because the children are confined to wheelchairs, have their heads harnessed so they can't bang them against walls or hard objects, and wear mouthpieces so that they don't chew on their tongues or lips. It is a cruel disease. Most die by the time they are age fifteen due to organ failure.

Maggie said simply, "Nobody applied so I figured I could do it." And my heart swelled with awe and wonder and the greatest admiration and love. It is hard to fall out of love with a person like that. Day after day, Maggie would come home from work with her stories, spoken sometimes with a smile and sometimes with tears, of caring for Raymond, who had been given such a tough hand to play in life. It wasn't long before Raymond loved her. As the medical manuals predicted, he died just before his seventeenth birthday.

In our culture, way too much is made of the link between passion and physical appearance, and far too little is made of the link between selflessness and beauty. I have always found Maggie compelling and attractive, and a big part of that is her generosity, self-forgetfulness, and hospitality.

3. It is unhelpful to romanticize the work of caring about those who live on the street (or in a wheelchair); it is often very difficult. Loving your neighbor can be wonderfully satisfying or remarkably trying; it is usually both. As a young couple soon to be married, our experience of working with people who were homeless gave us a direct view into the nature of commitment and care. Love is not always a response to something attractive; in fact, as it matures, it's not a responsive action at all. It's a choice, a way of being, a recognition of a commonality that invites—no, *requires*—our investment in each other. It can be and is often trying.

As Maggie and I have walked together the very human path—including error, distractibility, and selfishness—the option of forgiveness has come more and more readily, birthed, in part, from the graced lessons we learned from trying to be neighbors to our abandoned sisters and brothers on the street. Recognizing the obvious woundedness that expresses itself as homelessness afforded Maggie and me the room to admit and embrace our own, less obvious wounds and each other's vulnerability. I think this made it more possible for us to forgive each other, probably the single biggest asset for a marriage and a necessary part of the journey of love. There's no option for love if we require perfection from each other. Maggie and I do not have a perfect relationship. Far from it. But we do have a relationship in which we forgive regularly.

Choosing to love is different from falling in love, but they're not unrelated. Choosing to love, to forgive, to be patient and kind even in a rough patch, as far as I can tell, is the most promising container in which falling in love can happen over and over. Laughter and joy are sustained only by commitment through tears and rupture.

4. Knowing what to say yes (amen) to also informs what to say no to. Believing that each of us is here only because of a divine generosity, and that every human life is precious, and that

we are therefore called, first and foremost, to tend to that gift of life, helped us to put other, unhelpful narratives in their place. For example, the idea that we human beings are primarily competitors, sparring in the pursuit of financial trophies, pales in comparison. To imagine that this gift of life should be spent in earning, collecting, and hoarding is intellectually insulting, environmentally disastrous, and spiritually bankrupt. Yet in the absence of a more compelling, very different vision, it can swallow up the human soul. Indeed, much of American politics and religion seems to worship at the altar of this lousy idea.

The practice of various forms of simplicity—which inherently includes a suspicion of consumption—has, perhaps paradoxically, en-"riched" our lives. I remember when we bought our first farm in Central Kentucky and the insurance agent asked what the "contents" of our house were worth. We went from room to room, closet to closet, did the math, and told him, "About one thousand dollars," which caused him to laugh skeptically. But we had done the math correctly; we had purchased the few things we owned at garage sales and thrift stores. And while it makes life easier to travel lightly, the real benefit of simplicity is to direct one's attention to relationship. Instead of being distracted by stuff and its upkeep and protection, there is the liberating space to focus only on relationship. One of my favorite memories of living in our nonelectrified, straw-bale home on the farm was that we would light the house with oil lamps and candles. In the darkness of late evening, sitting at a table with only candlelight in the center of the table, meant that Maggie and I and our daughters would talk, and all that we could really see was each other's face. With no telephone or TV (and before computers and cell phones), it was hard to get distracted.

One of the common factors that often results in divorce is financial pressure caused by overspending by one or both spouses. A shared commitment to simplicity can help reduce financial worries. Marriage is hard enough without arguing about the credit card bill and being anxious about mounting debt. Over the years, Maggie and I have crafted little competitions about who can spend less; she usually wins. But the happy reality is that we have never really been troubled about money, even when we didn't have much of it.

However, as I write these words, I am reminded that in millions of homes all over the world, there is nothing close to one thousand dollars worth of stuff. I am aware that the definition of simplicity for North Americans is a far cry from what it could be, perhaps what it ought to be. Maggie and I continue to explore and wrestle with the demands of simplicity. To reduce our carbon footprint, we now have solar panels on our home, drive a salvaged electric car, dry our clothes on a line, and still grow a lot of our own food. But we are aware that we could do even more.

5. Having a missionally oriented marriage meant, not surprisingly, missionally oriented parenting. Maggie and I had a sense of how we wanted to raise our children and what we might hope for them. Yes, we made loads of mistakes and we carried a lot of cultural baggage and blindness through it all; I still bear a lot of regret about what I might have done differently. On the other hand, we knew we wanted to raise our children into generosity, into compassion, into a wide embrace.

One of the odd and ironic aspects of raising children with a gospel orientation is that we Christians invest ourselves as parents in the care of these little human beings, protecting them from harm, with the ultimate and ironic hope that they become adults who can love generously, even putting themselves in harm's way for that cause. So goes the paradox of love. For example, when one of our daughters had the opportunity to travel to Haiti as a high school student, we considered the physical risk and the likely spiritual deepening (*encuentro*) and we encouraged her to go. She went, we worried, and she was significantly impacted by the experience. When another daughter was invited to an out-of-state Habitat for Humanity experience for young people that would require her to experience the difficult, impoverished living conditions of a big part of the world, we urged her to participate. She went, we worried, and she learned a lot. When yet another daughter was afforded the opportunity to travel to a very poor community in Cambodia, we made sure that it would happen. She went, we worried, and it was a powerful experience for her. Even while we worried, these kinds of experiences were important to us.

Along the way, we worked hard as parents to downplay wealth and possessions, to resist the rise of the cell phone culture, to highlight the importance of caring for vulnerable people and caring for the earth, and importantly, to love our daughters with determination and patience. We were not extraordinary parents. But, happily, today we share a wonderful comradery with each of our now adult daughters. Maggie and I admire their choices and their generosity, and we love just to be with them.

6. The final testimony I can offer is that it has been such a good life with Maggie. I have often reflected on the paradoxical promise of faith: we gain our lives by losing them. We gain our lives by giving them away. To say it another way, we discover life and meaning and love and deepest satisfaction and the sacred by investing ourselves in the good of others, including and necessarily with those who are in harm's way. This gospel promise, I believe, is at the heart of what it means to be a whole and holy human being. As such, it is a message for all people, married and unmarried. Maggie and I together aspired to make this message our own. All I can say is that it is hard to imagine another message that would have been as life-giving. To aspire to a missional life has meant that I have tried to invest my life in one way or another in the good of others, including Maggie, especially Maggie, but not only Maggie.

Maggie and I see each other not only as someone we care about but someone we care *with*. We are a partnership in the name of love, mercy, generosity. We frequently fall short, but at least we know who we are trying to be.

My hunch and observation are that when couples embrace this message and partnership together, there is a very good chance it will make their marriage better—richer, deeper, more life-giving, more satisfying, less distracted, more impactful, more thoughtful, more prayerful, more generative, more soulful—just better. People will stay together not out of obligation but out of a deeply held and shared vocation to bring hope and healing to the world.

It strikes me that the Catholic tradition has put a lot of emphasis on the indissolubility of marriage by trying to outlaw divorce, forbidding remarriage and offering the difficult process of annulment as a necessary way out of a broken relationship. All of this is done in the name of supporting marriage and its aspiration of a lifetime commitment.

May I propose, alternatively, that a missional orientation to marriage supplies the distinctive content that would inspire and empower people to make a commitment to each other, to the world, and to their faith that honors the gospel invitation and the hope of fidelity? If there is something truly distinctive about Christian marriage, it's not that it just lasts a lifetime. Many selfish and/or unhappy people have managed to stay married until one or the other dies. Rather, what is distinctive about Christian marriage is that it aims for a shared relationship that is so generous, so hospitable, and so broadly loving in the now that it flowers into a lifetime. If young people are to be convinced that a lifetime commitment is better than "living together" (which is to describe a relationship in the most uninspiring, unimaginative way possible), it will be because of the distinctive quality of a shared, committed mission. When we get so happily tangled up in the teamwork of loving the world together, it is hard to imagine walking away from that communion.

Preparing for a Missional Marriage

With this vision of a missional marriage in mind, how then might we rethink the marriage preparation that is offered in our parish communities? Of course, the first observation is that it must flow from the faith community from which it comes. In other words, if marriage and marriage prep are to have a missional flavor, it should be because the parish has that missional flavor or, at least, missional aspiration.

When a parish is distinctively and decisively committed to relationship with those who are poor, homeless, abandoned, sick, or vulnerable, then its members will be encouraged and commissioned and equipped to be engaged. These experiences, as I have mentioned in previous chapters, will change them. They will want to continue in the footsteps of Jesus, St. Francis, and Dorothy Day—the footsteps of hope, healing, and compassion. That is the ideal. So, practically, whatever the parish does, organizes, and offers also creates contexts in which people meet as potential friends or spouses. If people meet while doing the work of compassion and justice, it serves to frame how they think about each other, their relationships, and their future together.

Of course, the reality is that people will continue to meet in all kinds of places (or at websites) with various degrees of interest in their faith, and many will continue to come to the parish seeking to get married. What, then, might an introduction to a missional marriage look like?

Very simply, marriage prep should involve those to be married in experiences that might open their eyes and their hearts and speak to a vision of a marriage *vocation* that looks beyond just the two of them. Couples to be married could be invited, as part of their preparation for marriage, to serve every week for three months at the local soup kitchen, visit the sick at the hospital, participate in St. Vincent de Paul home visits, accompany a new refugee family through the local Catholic Charities, or any combination or all of them. Couples should be mentored not only by people who have managed to be married for a while but especially by people who are married and who share a mission of generosity, justice, and care for the wider community. The important message to be communicated is that marriage has the potential to be a partnership with and for a vision.

Yes, of course, there needs to be more detail to this strategy, but the point is that most of marriage preparation must look very different than it currently does.

We have a duty and a responsibility as keepers of this faith tradition to share it, even as it might challenge. People who are getting married—indeed all people—deserve the benefit of knowing that there is this loving/missional option for their lives and for their relationships, not as a matter of saving them from some eternal hell, but to discourage them from living a lesser life. The power and pleasure of marriage must not be short-changed by a lesser vision. To put it positively, we believe that life and love and marriage can be so very good, but especially when they honor the sacred linkage that makes *all of us* family.

Being married with Maggie has been the best part of my life. Sharing a mission of love—our modest attempt at a compassion duet—has been our way of experiencing marriage as a vocation, and a life-giving and joyful one at that.

6

The Heart of Mission and Parish Renewal

An Option for the Poor

In February 1977 a conservative priest was named archbishop in a small Latin American country. A modest and good man, he was mostly inclined toward books and theological study. Little of significance was expected of him.

Within a few months, his responsibility for a war-torn country full of poor people changed him. In his conversion, Archbishop Oscar Romero recognized the tragedy and devastation of the poverty of his native El Salvador. He saw with new eyes children dying of chronic diarrhea and villages devastated by malnutrition, joblessness, hopelessness, and government-sponsored violence.

His skilled mind enabled him to quickly identify the true causes—the spiritual, political, and economic causes—that were the ruin of many of his fellow Salvadorans. He would spend the rest of his life—a life shortened by an assassin's bullet—in the service of the poor, offering support and care, challenging the political and economic forces that exploited them, and speaking a word of hope and reconciliation.

But this is not just a story about the heroic witness of a very holy man; what happened to Archbishop Oscar Romero reveals and proclaims what it means to be Catholic, what it means to be neighbor, and what it means to be parish. If our eyes are open and our hearts are wide, we can and will be tugged by the despair and abandonment of others away from our books and comfort to people, places, and positions unfamiliar and difficult. We might even spend—literally spend—our lives in the service of that tug.

We are, we believe, made in the image of God. But what does that mean? Consider this: if we are indeed made in the image of God, it is a God whose call to Moses was motivated by the suffering and despair of a group of slaves. If we are made in the image of God, it is a God who, in the person of Jesus, noticed and responded to the desperation of the sick, the poor, the stranger, the broken. In other words, if we are made in the image of God, we are made for each other, with a predisposition to care about one another's lives. That predisposition intensifies around suffering.

The Power of a Phrase

Archbishop Romero's story and transformation did not happen in a vacuum. In 1979 the Latin American bishops, including Romero, met in Puebla, Mexico, to address the affairs and direction of the Catholic Church in Latin America and issued a statement that included the following: "From the heart of Latin America, a cry rises to the heavens ever louder and more imperative. It is the cry of a people who suffer." The most popular and powerful effect of the document issued from the 1979 Puebla General Conference has been the impact of a simple, six-word phrase. The bishops titled one of the key sections of their document "The Preferential Option for the Poor," and that single phrase has provoked and informed the larger church's social imagination.

When the Latin American bishops met in Puebla, and before that in Medellín, Colombia, in 1968, the predominant experience of the larger church there was poverty. As the bishops wrote in the earlier document from Medellín, "[We] cannot remain indifferent in the face of the tremendous social injustice existent in Latin America, which keeps the majority of our people in dismal poverty, which in many cases becomes inhuman wretchedness." "Dismal poverty" and "inhuman wretchedness" were filling the pews of the churches in poor communities. Either the church would have to address these realities or cease to be credible. The preferential option for the poor portrays a serious, open-eyed, determined posture toward the problem of poverty.

The bishops at Puebla and Medellín were having to negotiate not only the fact of widespread deprivation and desperation but a legacy of disinterest and even disdain for the poor. In her momentous book *Cry of the People*, Penny Lernoux chronicles the legacy of the Catholic magisterium in Latin America until the middle of the twentieth century. The leadership of the church, Lernoux wrote, "[had] encouraged a deep strain of cynicism among the upper classes, who learned that they might do anything, including slaughter innocent peasants, as long as they went to Mass, contributed land and money to the church's aggrandizement, and baptized their children. These were the 'good Christians' honored by the Latin American Bishops."

The bishops, wanting to break with the past, were put in the challenging position of having to assume the role of prophet. They needed to speak a fresh word that not only expressed an authentic commitment by church leadership to the majority poor of their countries but that also opened the affluent eyes of those blind to the suffering and that encouraged broader commitment to the poor among church membership.

The bishops, priests, and lay leaders did their job well. The transformation of many parts of the Latin American church during the 1970s, '80s, and '90s bordered on the miraculous. And the

adaptation of the preferential option for the poor by other confer-
ences of bishops, popes, and theologians as well as other Christian
traditions is testimony to the provocative power of the phrase and
the action that it prompted.

One reason the phrase has received such attention is its
theological and biblical soundness. As Latin Americans and their
pastors looked to the Bible for answers to landlessness and oppression, the exodus story came alive with its account of a people being
liberated from slavery and brought to a land they could call their
own, a place where justice could reign. As Latin American peasants encountered the words of the prophets, they heard of a God
whose care seemed particularly committed to those in anguish and
whose wrath seemed reserved for the powerful and wealthy. In
other words, God cared about them *and* cared about a solution to
their problems. As *campesina* widows, whose husbands had been
tortured and killed by government forces, gathered to study Jesus's
words about the reign of God, Jesus's actions on behalf of the poor
and suffering, and even his cause of death, they encountered a person poor like themselves, a man who yearned for reconciliation
between privilege and poverty, one whose commitment to the
dignity of all and the liberation of the poor was of such passion
and importance that he was willing to die for those convictions—a
man who, we believe, was the Son of God. The German theologian
Jürgen Moltmann has observed, "Reading the Bible with the eyes
of the poor is a different thing from reading it with a full belly. If it
is read in the light of the experience and hopes of the oppressed,
the Bible's revolutionary themes—promise, exodus, resurrection
and spirit—come alive."

Significantly, when the US Catholic bishops issued their
pastoral on the economy only seven years later in 1986, they
referred to the preferential option for the poor as a touchstone for
their writing, applying it for the first time to the situation in the

United States. Furthermore, in their important but underutilized 1994 document on the social mission of the parish, titled *Communities of Salt and Light*, the US bishops again refer to the phrase. They go on to state boldly and unambiguously, "Our parish communities are measured by how they serve 'the least of these' in our parish and beyond its boundaries—the hungry, the homeless, the sick, those in prison, the stranger."

It is difficult to find a book written in the last forty years addressing the topic of Catholic (or Christian) response to injustice and poverty that does not mention or elaborate on the phrase. John Paul II was the first pope to employ and adapt the phrase when he talked about a "preferential love of the poor."

The ongoing testimony of the power of this phrase is that it essentially defines most of the critical commitments of Pope Francis. From the selection of his name, Francis (as in Francis of Assisi), a saint known for his commitment to the poor, to his simple lifestyle, to the pastoral focus of his travels, to his declaration of a "Year of Mercy," and to the constancy of his words on care of and "tenderness" for the poor and vulnerable, will forever be remembered for his championing the preferential option for the poor. In many ways, Pope Francis never even needs to speak the phrase verbatim because it is so profoundly infused in everything he does.

What Is a "Preferential Option for the Poor"?

While theologians may differ on some aspects of the meaning of the phrase, it is safe to highlight a few critical characteristics of the preferential option for the poor.

1. *The preferential option for the poor is fundamental and scriptural.* The option for the poor is reflected in—you could even say *advocated by*—God in Scripture. While that might be startling at first, the preferential option for the poor is, in fact, a responsible,

reasonable way to describe the stories of Yahweh's activity in the biblical narrative. That is, it is a valid description of the call of Moses and the liberation of the Hebrew people from Egypt in the book of Exodus. It is an accurate portrayal of the Old Testament prophets and their concern for the care of widows, orphans, and foreigners. Perhaps most important for Christians, it is a truthful description of the ministry of Jesus, whose care and teaching demonstrated an obvious dedication to the weak and neglected.

One caution: God does not love poor people more than rich people. But the love of God gets focused in a particular way on those who suffer. This is not unfamiliar to us: imagine the love of parents when one of their children is seriously sick. They dedicate themselves to the recovery of the sick child with special and deliberate care, all the while not loving any less their healthy children. So it is with God. God's preferential love for the poor is motivated both by their pain and by divine intention that all of us live lives of dignity.

2. *The preferential option for the poor has a goal.* It does not assent to the position that poverty is inevitable or acceptable. The meaningfulness of love is that it makes a felt and observable difference. Love that pours itself out for the poor ultimately desires the end of the suffering and, therefore, seeks an end to the *cause* of the suffering.

There is nothing in the logic of the gospel that suggests that God wants some people to be well-fed and others to die of starvation. On the contrary, the very claim that God is creator of all has within it the assumption that everyone is a child of God, and, as such, is precious and valuable. Poverty is not a condition to be tolerated. Period.

Those of us with wealth must do more than share our money and possessions with those who have less or little. Yes, of course, share, but the hope and dream underneath any kind of generosity is that all our sisters and brothers will know a dignified life. A life of dignity is one that has daily access to housing, food, health care, and work opportunities, as well as civic participation and religious freedom. Our call to compassion is not exhausted by addressing, even generously, an emergency need for jackets or shoes. We are called to communion, community, right relationships, justice. We seek to make all things right.

3. *The preferential option for the poor is multidimensional.* A healthy, integrated care for the poor necessarily expresses itself in myriad ways, including the solidarity of friendship and accompaniment as well as the familiar and important expressions of charity: donations, soup kitchens, homeless shelters, and emergency assistance. Moreover, a holy determination to ease or eliminate poverty will ultimately evolve into the recognition of and engagement with the political and economic forces at play. Our pope knows this; our bishops know this; Catholic Charities USA knows this; the Society of St. Vincent de Paul knows this. Those who experience poverty know this. As Catholic social teaching boldly proclaims, our faith has political consequences.

Indeed, both the Mosaic covenant and Jesus's notion of the reign of God address realities that speak to the influence that faith has on politics. The ministry of Moses, motivated by God's love for the Hebrew slaves but obstructed by the designs of the pharaoh, was necessarily political and revolutionary. Similarly, Jesus's proclamations of the "year of God's favor" and "reign of God" were challenging words at a time when the oppressive "reign of pharaoh" was not to be questioned. For much of the poor, "a land of milk and honey" or the "reign of God" can only be understood in the light of faith and their implication for all human endeavor, including politics.

It is certainly true that some forms of human brokenness and suffering are not matters of politics, such as the suffering caused by tornadoes or illness. However—and this is critical—poverty almost always is. Most of the poor are poor because of exploitative political and economic forces beyond their control. Period.

4. *The preferential option for the poor navigates the phenomenon called sin.* Donal Dorr's book *Option for the Poor*, the first version of which was written only four years after the 1979 Puebla General Conference, analyzes the history of Catholic social teaching as it concerns itself specifically with the option for the poor. Historically, he observes, the Church's teaching has been persistent in its statement of caring for the poor and its call of conversion and responsibility to the rich. However, the Church has not been nearly as helpful in counseling the poor when faced with an unrepentant oppressor, a pharaoh (or a group of pharaohs) if you will. Political and economic decisions—as Moses, the prophets, and Jesus recognized—often pay homage to the selfish interests of the powerful at the expense of the well-being of others. The blindness of the rich and powerful is one particularly virulent version of sin.

A preferential option for the poor calls us to stand on the side of those whose lives have been diminished by neglect or scarcity. This means we stand, not as enemies of anyone, but as allies of the poor and as adversaries of the political decisions and sinful realities that rob them of life. Specifically, this means that if we must make a choice between the political preferences of those who have (more than) enough and political solutions for those who do not, we opt to stand with those who are struggling with deprivation.

5. *A preferential option for the poor is based on faith.* While a preferential option for the poor may express itself in political and economic, as well as civic and charitable ways, it is ultimately a matter of faith. "Preferential option for the poor" names the size of God's heart and the concomitant claim on our own hearts. It names our willingness to suffer and sacrifice and endure hardship

on behalf of our sisters and brothers. After all, what can holiness mean in our faith tradition except that we become people whose love grows and grows to include the care of all? And what would our love and faith mean if we did not seek out and care for the most wounded among us? As Dorothy Day once wrote, "We love God only as much as we love the person whom we love the least." Or, as Jesus speaks it, "Whatever you did to the least of these, you did to me."

Six Things You and Your Parish Can Do

What might a preferential option for the poor mean in our own lives? I will assume for a moment that most readers are of relative privilege. Father Jon Sobrino, SJ, writes that there are two classes of people in the world: rich and poor. The rich do not worry about whether they will eat tomorrow; the poor do. So, we must accept that most of us reading this are rich. Given our privileged status, how do we integrate a preferential option for the poor into our lives? Here I try to be as practical as possible.

If you grew up like me, it's possible that you never thought much about poverty, or at least you haven't thought about it other than to wish it didn't exist. Here's my confession: I am the son of parents who managed to become relatively wealthy. My youth was spent in the contemplation of tennis and water skiing. I spent seven hundred dollars my first semester in college just on eating out. My capacity for distraction and self-preoccupation is vast. So, if you are half the scoundrel I am, consider these possibilities.

First, it is important, as Pope Francis says, to "draw near," to *be directly connected to someone who is poor*, and to come to know even tenderness for someone on the margins. I didn't really care a thing about the world's poor until I cared about one poor person. And I only came to care about one poor person because I put myself in a place where that could happen. In my case, it happened at a day shelter for the homeless. Tom and I played cards, drank coffee, and just talked. After a month or so, I stopped being fearful of Tom and started to like him. And, despite my many quirks, Tom seemed to like me. Most important, I heard Tom's story. I heard the story of his difficult life, as well as his hopes and dreams, and it changed me some. I have had other such encounters since then, with people in Central America and with folks who experience poverty in both urban and rural settings in this country. All these encounters changed me as well. But the point is that we need at least to give ourselves a face-to-face opportunity to care about somebody who's poor, somebody a lot of us probably wouldn't even see in the course of a normal day.

So, spend some time with an abandoned elderly person at a nursing home or serve and eat lunch with the guest of a soup kitchen. Become a big brother or big sister to a child growing up in inner-city poverty or in a rural shack with only one parent. Pope Francis calls it *encuentro*, or encounter. These encounters change us, steer us, and form us.

Practically and programmatically, what this means for parishes is that they should become places that organize, plan, and facilitate deliberate encounters between rich and poor.

Second, *begin to ask questions and search for answers*. After the first step, a face-to-face encounter may stimulate an appetite for information or education. As I continued to work at the soup kitchen as a young man, I started to ask myself, *Why are half the men here Vietnam vets?* I wanted to know why a great many of the visitors at the soup kitchen were mentally ill, and I wanted to know what opportunities were available to them.

These are simply the questions that come to us when we care about somebody else. And perhaps they stimulate larger questions about poverty: Why are some people unable to escape the projects? Why are there projects? Should we be helping people escape them, or should we be helping low-income communities recover and prosper? Why are the people of El Salvador unable to feed themselves? Why do Third World countries export food when their own people are starving?

Many of the realities that plague the human family are not immediately or quickly understood. It is critical that we take the time and effort to invest ourselves in relationships with those who suffer and to commit ourselves to the research that might yield greater understanding. If we want to solve problems, it is important that we do the proper study. This work might sometimes seem dry, hard, and overly academic, but its inspiration is love.

It is true—*mea culpa, mea culpa*—I probably spend too much time reading the sports page and gardening catalogs, but because of the encounters I've had with my fellow human beings who experience poverty, I also read the news from Bread for the World or Catholic Relief Services or the website of the Maryknoll Office for Global Concerns. Yes, sometimes it is difficult, but I can't and won't stop. It would be at this point in my life like abandoning my heart and faith—not to mention my blood relatives on the margins.

Throughout this book I have repeatedly referred to some important mission-based organizations. Almost all of them offer lots of very good resources describing many kinds of human crises and the actions addressing those crises. I consider these kinds of educational resources to be the proper companion to whatever prayer resources any one of us might use. It's hard to know what to pray for or how to pray if we're not aware of what's happening on this earth, our home.

What this means is that parishes must be deliberate about thinking of the human condition and social realities as part of what it means to educate a community of faith. Understanding the world around us—both its wounds and its wonders—is (or should be) an important part of Christian education.

Third, *start to advocate*. As we become more aware of the causes and possible solutions to the crises that burden our sisters and brothers nearby and faraway, it is very important that we become advocates for the healing of the political and economic relationships and policies that are broken. We can spend all the time we want at soup kitchens, but unless something changes, the one thing that we will probably notice is that there are more and more people showing up every week. We need to ask ourselves, *So what's going on that makes the soup kitchen such a popular place these days? How are we going to fix an economy in which the gap between rich and poor continues to grow? How can I help? And how can non-profit groups, businesses, the Church, and the government help?*

It is critical that our faith and our love move us into political participation and political responsibility. Might not religious education, ministry formation, Confirmation classes, and the RCIA want to prepare blossoming Catholics for such a task? And for us old Catholics who have not been trained for such and who feel unprepared, we might simply have to take a deep breath and jump in.

I was giving a talk on Catholic social teaching at a parish in Connecticut many years ago, during which I began to discuss the importance for Catholics and all Christians to take the values of their faith into the political conversation. I hadn't gotten very far when a middle-aged man stood up and interrupted me somewhat angrily, saying, "I've been a devoted Catholic all of my life and I've never found it necessary to sully my faith with politics!" I was considering my response, when almost immediately a physically tiny, elderly woman with fiery eyes and set chin, replied in her broken German accent, "If you do not take your faith into politics, you too will end up with a man like Hitler." Then she sat down, and I didn't really need to say anything more.

Almost as dramatic, Bread for the World, a great and potent Christian organization (which you can join) that lobbies in Washington on hunger and poverty issues, estimates that for every letter written on behalf of antihunger legislation, a life is saved. One letter written = one life saved! Have I something better to do with my time?

Again, the parish must become a place where public life and political engagement are taken seriously. For example, the parish could and should be the place where civil and respectful conversation can be had among differing voices. The parish should be a place where serious attention is given to the issues affecting the poor and vulnerable and should empower its members to act. The parish should even be a place, taking the advice of Pope Francis, where people of faith and integrity with particular skills are encouraged by the parish community to run for political office.

A fourth expression of the preferential option for the poor will see us *working side by side with those who are poor as they help themselves.* This is what we might call solidarity work and/or community organizing. As we move into (1) relationships, (2) education, and (3) advocacy, sooner or later we will probably arrive at the realization that the very best way forward is to work in partnership.

It is powerful and exciting to be part of a process or project that includes people of various economic backgrounds working together on a common purpose with shared hopes and convictions. In this scenario, the means speak to and instill the ends: people working together, caring about each other's welfare, and filled with hope. That's the world we seek and that's how this work gets done. This is the work that the Catholic Campaign for Human Development (CCHD), an antipoverty program, has encouraged and funded for many years. The CCHD website offers this compelling self-description: "The belief that those who are directly affected by unjust systems and structures have the best insight into knowing how to change them is central to CCHD. CCHD works to break the cycle of poverty by helping low-income people participate in decisions that affect their lives, families and communities."[1]

In cities where the work of CCHD or faith-based community organizing is present, parishes could and should encourage a committee of passionate members to link with CCHD and organize the parish around opportunities to support its work in the community.

Fifth, *share your resources.* While your presence and effort are invaluable, do not underestimate the additional potency of sharing your wealth. Good work needs resources to fuel its potential impact. So, give your money! The early Christian definition of "disposable income" was that it is the rightful possession of the poor. Like all things, the key is to just to get started. Decide that you are going to give away 25 percent, 10 percent, 5 percent, 1 percent, or .001 percent of your income and just do it. Then periodically and prayerfully consider if the amount is still suitable or needs to be adjusted.

Let me suggest that you earmark some of your tithe for local causes, some for international causes, and some for person-to-person support. Just remember that giving money does not replace relationship; in the words of St. Vincent de Paul, "The poor will forgive your gifts of food only by feeling your love."

Pastors and staffs (and business managers!) might be reluctant to encourage parishioners to give generously to other organizations, worrying that doing so might result in decreased giving to the parish. In fact, the results are often just the opposite. When the parish links people in meaningful relationships with important and impactful organizations doing important things in this world,

---

[1] http://www.usccb.org/about/catholic-campaign-for-human-development/.

parishioners only become fonder of, more grateful for—and supportive of—their parish. Many pastors, after linking their parishioners with some important work or cause, have described to me how those same parishioners significantly and simultaneously increased their giving to the parish as a consequence.

The sixth and final point is that the option for the poor and vulnerable is something that we do best together; in many ways, that is the theme of this book. *The work of compassion, to make an option for the poor, is most effectively and faithfully done in packs.* We must do this work together; if not, we fall prey to burnout, cynicism, recklessness, or the tyranny of our own egos. Working together makes it possible to share joy and struggle in a way that makes us whole. My most stubbornly held dream is that one day all parishes and churches will see to it that every member is formed and encouraged in the tradition of the option for the poor and that parishes will be divided up into mission teams that, *together*, explore ways to make a difference in the lives of our sisters and brothers who are poor.

The heart of this option for the poor is the insistence that love, generosity, compassion, and justice are the manifestations of God's heart and truest expression of our humanity. The option for the poor is just a reminder of who we are—a people who, when we are open and awake, would do anything to end one another's suffering and see joy abound.

7

Culturing Peace and Justice

A Recipe for the Peacemaking Parish

If you want yogurt, you must culture milk with exactly the right bacteria (specifically, *Lactobacillus bulgaricus* and *Streptococcus thermophilus*). If you want violence, you must culture the world with exactly the right ingredients or, more correctly, exactly the wrong ingredients. If we have a culture of violence, it is because we human beings have cultured violence. We have created it. It is not a surprise. It is not random. It is the predictable consequence of a recipe we have attached ourselves to and carried out. That is both bad news and good news. The bad news is that we are responsible. The good news is that we can choose a different recipe. The good news is called the reign of God. And the reign of God is at hand. It is at hand. It is for the picking. It is for the choosing.

From Syria to Tibet, Iraq to Myanmar, Charleston to Orlando, there is the upheaval and wound called violence; it looks overwhelming sometimes. But the first and last word is a holy word called *hope*—not hope like optimism that everything will turn out fine; we already know that that is not true. The snuffed-out lives of starving or bombed or abandoned people every day says very clearly that everything in this world does not turn out fine. Rather, the hope I am describing is the hope of our faith that says that there are things worth living for, things that give life—and they are love, reconciliation, compassion, justice, peace, solidarity, and healing. We can see through the lens of hope, perhaps with fresh eyes, that Jesus *is*, in fact and in a very practical way, the savior of the world. If we do not heed his message, we will perish. *And,* if we have indeed crafted a world—perhaps blindly—that is at risk and in crisis, hope tells us we can live a different way and there can be healing and there can be a new possibility. It is possible, instead of culturing violence, for us to culture peace.

A world that knows violence needs the message and work of its opposite, nonviolence. As Pope Francis stated in his January 2017 message on the occasion of the fiftieth World Day of Peace Celebration, "To be true followers of Jesus today also includes embracing his teaching about nonviolence." Since most Catholic followers of Jesus consider their spiritual home the local parish, it stands to reason that if the work of Catholic peacemaking is to grow, it will do so because—and perhaps only because—it thrives and flourishes in the parish. If we want to see something Catholic grow, it must root itself in the parish. Period. That observation colors everything that follows.

By the notion of "culturing peace," I intend it to have double meaning. First, borrowing from the biological definition of "culturing," I want to suggest that we need to identify all the right ingredients and commit ourselves to the full mix of the right ingredients to allow peace to happen. That is, what range of commitments must we make to see an outcome like peace? And second, borrowing from the sociological definition of "culture," we need to deliberately apply ourselves to what makes for culture, human culture, and how to apply the knowledge of that to crafting a *holy* human culture.

To return to the first point, I am borrowing loosely from the biological meaning of culturing, as in culturing yogurt or penicillin

—essentially, what ingredients, what conditions must be present in the mixture for something to grow. You cannot make yogurt without critical ingredients: milk and two kinds of bacteria. If you do not have those two ingredients, there can be no fermentation and there will be no yogurt. Our interest, of course, is to define the ingredients that make for peace. What ingredients *must* be present in the community of faith for it to become a truly effective agent of peace? Because, if they are not all there, we can do all kinds of good things but, in the absence of the full slate of required ingredients, there will be no peace.

The huge advantage of situating the work of peace in the parish is that while all the various ingredients must be present in the parish as part of the community's vocabulary and missional touchstones, not everyone has to do everything; in fact, no one can possibly do everything. What is critical is that all the ingredients are present and celebrated and dynamically inform each other within the Body of Christ called the parish. In addition, the parish enjoys the profound benefit of the catalytic ingredients of friendship, affection, and intimacy that make the work of peacemaking more integral and compelling.

So, first things first. This probably goes without saying, but to draw from Pope Paul VI's famous words, there will be no peace without justice. The relationship between peace and justice is that they are so closely tied together—theologically and practically—that it is nearly impossible to speak of one without the other. Having said that, then, the question restated is as follows: What ingredients must be present for an outcome that looks like peace *and* justice, peace *with* justice, justice that *flows into* peace?

I want to describe six critical elements that *must* be present for there to be peace. We say we want peace, we might even work—and work very hard—for peace. However, if all the necessary ingredients are not present in our collective life as a faith community, the recipe simply cannot make for peace. I believe we sincerely desire peace, and therefore we must not do it in a sloppy or lazy fashion. We must become more scientific, more exact, about this work of our heart, so that we do not invite each other into endless frustration and disappointment.

First, *the Church—all of us—must always be deliberate about our relationships with those who are at risk in the world.* Catholic social teaching describes this, in part, as the "option for the poor and vulnerable" and as "solidarity." I begin here not because the Catholic tradition needs convincing but because our parishes do. It is my experience of doing social ministry for the last thirty-five years that the single biggest obstacle to the Church's mission and vision of peace with justice is the fact of the segregation of the poor/oppressed/exploited/neglected/stranger from the comfortable/secure/wealthy/satisfied. The result is a common but catastrophic divide that deceives the comfortable and secure that all is well and convinces the poor that there is no hope. The long-term result is death—dead bodies and dead dreams by starvation, drive-by shootings, desperation, and war, *and* dead souls and dead hearts by self-preoccupation and oversatiation. Apart and together they create what looks like real hell.

Let me direct my words for a moment to those readers who come from communities that are somewhat comfortable or even affluent: every one of us, regardless of what else we do, must try to stay connected face-to-face with the persons and the places at risk. The single biggest obstacle to the work of justice and peace is not militarism, nor consumerism, nor political ideology. Those are all obstacles, to be sure, but they are simply symptoms of a bigger obstacle. The biggest obstacle is the absence of authentic compassion, a derivative of *agape*. I will say it bluntly: it is very possible for people, including people of faith, not to care about each other. It sounds harsh, but it is not meant as an indictment.

It is simply an observation. So many of us do not really care about each other. And we do not care, I think, not because we are malicious or unfeeling or mean but because we simply do not see each other. Our lives, our cities are all crafted like subtle apartheids: all the rich people live with rich people, all the middle-class people live with middle-class people, and the poor live with the poor in the places left behind. So we do not care, perhaps we cannot care, about what we do not see and do not know.

Several years ago, I was in Greenville, South Carolina, listening to a group of folks from a wealthy church who had recently participated in a poverty tour of their own city, driving on the streets of Greenville's poorest neighborhoods. Some mentioned with distress and sadness and even shock that they had lived in Greenville all their lives and never knew how desperately poor parts of the city were. *But*—this is important—having seen those places, having prayed at those places, having considered those places through the lens of faith, most of them were obviously *changed*. Now they *cared*. And their care now drives them into the first steps of active engagement.

Fr. Greg Boyle, a Jesuit priest who works with gangs in Los Angeles and is one of the most faithful and holy people I have ever been in the presence of, makes this observation: "There will be no peace without justice," restating the familiar words of Pope Paul VI. "But," he goes on, "there will be no justice without kinship." We will not know what needs to be done in this world without seeing the world through the lens of those who see it from the bottom. There will be no justice without kinship. There will be no peace without kinship. Perhaps this is why so many of our greatest peacemakers choose to be with and among the poor. It is not enough for the church to sit at our computers in suburbia, clicking on every good message to a member of Congress. The reign of God is critically relational. We must be connected in real life in real time. We learn much about God by looking into the eyes of the poor and vulnerable. And we discover that the world is much different than we thought. We learn that the world is a difficult place for many. And we discover that we have a capacity—a holy capacity—to love bigger than we might have dreamed.

Our work for peace must be linked integrally with the experience of those on the bottom. Only when they know peace will peace be. *As long as poverty is, violence will be.* On a practical level, the recipe for peace for those of us who live and pray in comfortable, even affluent churches must include a commitment to connect ourselves with those at the margins and a deliberate strategy of inviting others to *see* what they had not seen before. And we must hold each other accountable. If any one of us does not know well someone who is poor—cannot tell stories of conversation and interaction with someone who is poor—we are certainly missing an important ingredient for peace.

The second critical ingredient, which flows out of the first, *is what we sometimes call justice education.* It doesn't sound very sexy, but it really involves the matter of reclaiming our tradition as a Church. One remarkable appropriation of the biblical themes of justice is articulated in the language of Catholic social teaching. Catholic social teaching speaks to dignity, solidarity, the option for the poor, the rights of workers, care of creation, peace, and so on. It is, in fact, an extraordinary tradition. The problem is that it is so often not integrated in the educational life of the local faith community, the parish. It continues to be, to use a tiresome and now pathetic phrase, "our best-kept secret." Many, if not most, pastors today never studied Catholic social teaching while in seminary; many, if not most, catechists are unfamiliar with the tradition. It is possible and usual for people to go through Catholic grade school, Catholic high school, and Catholic college, Catholic youth group, the RCIA, Catholic spirituality programs, Catholic discipleship study groups and never encounter Catholic social teaching. And so often if they do, it is an afterthought, a kind of addendum or extracurricular activity. Thirty-five years ago, I spent three years at the University of Notre Dame getting a master of divinity degree. Most of my classmates were men preparing for priesthood. Guess how many courses in Catholic social teaching were required as part of the curriculum? Zero. Guess how many courses are required today, thirty-five years later? Zero.

I will say this: To the extent that people in the pews are not engaged with the poor, not involved in justice work, and not committed to active peacemaking is an indictment of almost every single expression of Catholic education and formation—from the seminaries and spirituality centers to Catholic colleges and preparation for First Communion.

On a very practical level, *we* must provide opportunities for our fellow Catholics to become educated. And when I say "we," I mean bishops and priests and deacons and religious and parishioners. Whatever category you fit in, when I say "we," I mean us: you and me.

We simply must be true to our tradition. We are really talking about the most critical work of naming what God we believe in. For many years at JustFaith Ministries, we offered a program called JusticeWalking for high school and college young people. It was so very heartening to see how engaged and excited young people can become about their faith when they hear it spoken through the lens of God's intimate care for the world, for the poor, for the stranger, for the vulnerable, for the enemy. Similarly, it sometimes surprised our staff to hear from JustFaith graduates who would remark that they had been away from the Church for years and that the experience of JustFaith is the reason that they came back to the parish. People want to know that Catholicism is a tradition that engages the critical needs and wounds of the world. The passion, vision, energy, and draw of the gospel await.

The third critical ingredient necessary for a culture of peace—and what may be the biggest challenge in the United States—is that *we must learn a new lifestyle, a simpler lifestyle.* As Wendell Berry puts it, "We must learn to live poorer than we do." The call to a simpler lifestyle is partially prompted by the observation that the world is at war because parts of the world are literally sucking the life out of the other parts. The history of affluence is the history of exploitation is the history of war. Rich lifestyles require the plunder of the earth, the cheap labor of other places, the poverty of others. Oil-inebriated lifestyles require a war in Iraq; there is no other way to put it. For us to live as we live in this country, we need to dominate others so that they cannot use the limited resources that we want for ourselves. As the author of the Epistle of James writes, "You want what you don't have, so you scheme and kill to get it" (4:2).

Our lifestyles not only put us at war with each other but with the natural order. The reality of climate change physically reminds us of the damage our lifestyles are doing. Again this year, in Louisville, Kentucky, where I live, another set of record high temperatures was established. The familiar sad images of polar bears drowning in the ocean or starving on land because their hunting grounds have simply melted under temperatures never before recorded is only one ominous warning of what most likely is to come, and not just to polar bears. On a practical level, we must reduce our ecological footprint, our level of consumption; I do not pretend to think that this will be easy. But to say we can't change is the excuse of the addict, says Berry. We can't continue to rely on that which will destroy us.

If the American lifestyle requires, on average, four times its share of the planet's resources, it is not enough to snip around the edges of our consumerism. It is not enough to thumb our noses at Walmart and shop enthusiastically everywhere else. We must learn how to reduce by three-quarters what we consume. We need to encourage each other to live in smaller homes, to buy less, to need less. Authentic love will not allow us to continue to ask the rest of the world to continue to put itself at the physical mercy of our conveniences. We will, I think, have to recover the language of sacrifice from our religious heritage. We simply cannot continue to draw from the booty of war and deprivation.

Some may argue that living a simpler life will not directly impact the wars in faraway places. In one sense, that is true. But if our lives say "more," then our lives say "war," and our words for peace become pious but empty gestures. As we peacemakers speak peace with our lips, our lifestyles must also speak peace.

The parish can become the place where conversations and education about how, to use the popular Mennonite phrase, "live more with less" happens. The parish can be the place where we assure one another that each of us is loved, even in the absence of designer labels on our clothes and late model cars. The parish can be the place where recycled clothing, cycling, and "staycations" (vs. exotic vacations) are celebrated and encouraged. The parish can continue to be the place that masters the perfect potluck—a simple way to celebrate each others' company with the best possible food!

The fourth ingredient for culturing peace is that *we must pray*. We must learn to pray. Then we must take the time to pray. Prayer has multiple meanings, hundreds of expressions, and a thousand functions. Prayer is a way of connecting with our Source, our God. It is about being centered, grounded, mindful of the holy and of the presence of the sacred and the precious. When I settle myself in the quiet and prayerful consideration of the reflections of Dorothy Day or Jean Vanier or Thomas Merton, I reconnect with what is most fundamental, true, and holy. The hope is for integration, singleness of purpose, openness to a deepening relationship and a deepening commitment.

Kathleen Norris describes prayer this way: "Prayer is not asking for what you think you want, but asking to be changed in ways you can't imagine." We must be people of prayer, people who are centered, people who draw from a deep well. When I am in the presence of prayerful people, I am always struck by the sense that they are drawing from a source of goodness that only comes from attentiveness to the deepest places in their hearts.

And, of course, the language of prayer is the language of spirituality. When my Protestant friends and I are trading denominational stories, they are often quick to mention the rich tradition of spirituality in the Catholic lexicon. Unfortunately, if Catholic social teaching is the best-kept secret in the Catholic Church, many of the traditions of spirituality are the second-best-kept secret. You just don't find enough of it at the local parish level.

My thought is that we must be as good at praying as we are at strategizing for the peace rally. Then the two will become linked. Prayerful people host prayerful rallies, engage in prayer-informed actions. Our work can become like a prayer—integrated, thoughtful, and wise.

The unpublicized benefit is that prayer can help us to connect with our poor neighbors with open eyes and hearts. Prayer can allow us to educate with patience, love, and understanding. Prayer can enable us to move to a simpler lifestyle. And prayer allows us to do this with conviction and joy.

Whether or not we pray is as obvious as whether or not we have put on our clothes. For example, the compulsive, frantic, angry, cynical, unintegrated rambling from project to project—even from peace project to peace project—may speak of good intentions, but an uneasy and untended inner life. It is possible—I have committed this sin—to do much harm even while trying to do good because we have not taken the time to pray. Untended hearts and spirits, like untended gardens, can go to weeds. Our good work for the world will be hampered if we do not do good work for our souls.

The fifth ingredient is a *commitment to nonviolence*. We must learn—as surely any serious consideration of Jesus's life and message will reveal—that God does not smile upon any form of violence. One benefit of a commitment to a nonviolent, peacemaking love is that the lens of peacemaking gives us a critical capacity for discernment. Consider the bombings of Hiroshima and Nagasaki: the presumption against violence frees us to see what the world so often wants to hide its eyes from. Violence is awful. Violence is ugly. Violence is the saddest of human acts. As John Paul II stated, "War is a defeat for humanity." And to the extent that any human institution relies on and promotes violence is the extent to which the Church must eye it suspiciously. Again, the point is discernment. Where is life honored? Where is it betrayed? It is so very difficult to lead people into a willing critique of their politics, their country, and their allegiances without some awareness of how violence is often the handmaid of greed and power.

Perhaps that is why nonviolence is so difficult for people in our country to consider. When we have so much, and so much to protect, violence becomes more and more necessary. On the other hand, when our things become few, when we genuinely care for the poor, the refugee, and the stranger here and abroad, when we know our tradition and have prayed well, the presumption of nonviolence becomes an obvious and necessary spiritual movement. Those who relied on violence in an earlier part of their lives often know a later regret that is very hard to heal.

Thus the prayer of the Church, the teaching of the Church, the practice of the Church must always bend in the direction of nonviolent action, more specifically nonviolent, loving action. We are nonviolent not because we simply eschew violence; rather, we are nonviolent because we are people who love, like Jesus. When our lives are active and occupied in the name of doing good, there is little space for violence and doing harm.

While the Church has historically held that in this complicated world some forms of defensive or protective violence seem, sadly, to be necessary, the presumption is that the threat and use of violence will always be a last and inadequate resort. If, to protect the innocent and vulnerable, for example, it becomes absolutely, unmistakably necessary to use force, it would be done with reluctance, heavy-heartedness, and carefulness. In other words, the just war theory can only make sense, and is only applicable, with the presumption against war and violence.

The sixth and most often overlooked ingredient of effective peacemaking is *community*. The historical template of our religious tradition is that so often those people most committed to peacemaking and justice were also people committed to community. There is a repeating pattern that suggests that the generativity of compassion and care that characterize a gospel life naturally issues into community. Big-heartedness always draws close to the other, always draws the other close. Francis of Assisi, St. Benedict, Dorothy Day, Jean Vanier—like Jesus himself—draw people naturally into relationship. And the hunger of the human heart that God created in us is not just for casual and recreational relationships. We long for relationships of meaning. We long to be connected, for healing, for vocation, and for mission.

Community might be the most neglected and daunting ingredient for us to embrace in the US context, and for the most obvious of reasons; we have come to worship at the altar of independence, individualism, and autonomy. As much as there is a deep hunger for connection, common purpose, and kindred hearts, there is a merciless, deep-rooted entrenchment in the forces of competition, freedom, and self-rule. We have, I fear, come to think of loneliness as necessary or inevitable.

The challenge before us, again, is to claim our tradition. From the description of the early Christian community in the Acts of the Apostles that "shared all things in common," to the early monastic families, to the development of the hundreds of canonical communities around the world, to the Catholic Worker communities of the twentieth and twenty-first centuries, to creation of parishes all over the world, Community 'R' Us.

The spiritual logic of local communities of faith is that they can live a smaller but living version of what they seek for the larger world. Communities of faith speak that peace is possible and seek to provide a living example, right here in our midst. It may not be perfect—it doesn't have to be—but it is a sign of how life can be nurtured and reverenced. The community of faith can be a place that witnesses to what is holy, good, loving, and life-giving by what it lives, by what it embodies. But like the other ingredients for peace mentioned so far, community is a commitment, a choice. And it involves effort, discipline, and struggle. It is certainly not easy.

As you might guess, when I say "community" I do not mean the bowling community or the coffee club; I mean the community of faith. I mean a parish community or a small faith community that embraces and celebrates very intentional commitments, including those I have mentioned so far: engagement with those on the margins, justice education or formation, simplicity, prayer, and peacemaking.

Even as small faith community movements and programs have become more and more popular across the country, most of the small faith communities I have witnessed at parishes have, unfortunately, been lacking in mission. They may pray, they may study, they may share a meal, but at the end of the day many of these communities dissolve simply because there was no mission that gave deeper meaning and purpose to their prayer and their learning and their fellowship. Small faith communities without a mission are just pious potlucks.

Our tradition suggests that it is very difficult to live a life of integrity apart from the support, encouragement, witness, challenge, and celebration of a community. Community is, if you will, the medium in which so many other important things of the gospel can happen. Community is an engine for peace; it is fuel for justice. We are made for each other. As a species, we have always known that we could not survive, could not flourish without each other. Whatever is to prosper, grow, or multiply will only happen with the nourishment of people who are *for* each other in a significant way.

I am interested to see many more forms of intentional community than what we see today, and I am interested to see the integration of intentional community within the parish. I would like to see the equivalent of Jesuit Volunteer Corps communities connected to every parish, where young people might commit to live for a term of two or three years, committed to the work of justice and peacemaking. I would like to see the parish encourage members to purchase homes near one another and in neighborhoods where there is greatest need, as an expression of the parish's work. I would like to see dioceses invite black and white and brown households into the faith-based mission of a covenant community, in which they meet weekly to explore where friendship and gospel love will take them and teach them. I would like to see some parishes sponsoring and supporting a L'Arche community. I am interested in the construction of simple homes, affordable and available for both poor and rich, to create neighborhoods where all can live and interact and be helpful to each other.

These six ingredients are essential elements of our faith tradition, essential elements of peacemaking: connection with those who suffer, the study of right relationships or peace and justice education, simple lifestyles, prayer, a commitment to nonviolence, and community. On one hand, they seem like just basic, standard ordinary gospel mandates. On the other hand, they represent significant challenges and opportunities for the local church, which has not typically focused itself on the matter of peace.

Finally, I would like to briefly address the matter of "culturing" peace, as in creating a human culture of peace. Our work to cultivate or culture peace means that there are times when we must be reactive; we must resist the forces of violence. This is frequently how the work of peacemaking presents itself: as the timely protest of some threat or expression of violence.

However, in addition, we must be proactive; we must *create* a human culture that speaks to peace and justice. We must imagine what God's peace and justice look like on this earth, and we must begin the work of crafting structures, institutions, and human realities that are the deliberate, purposeful, and institutionalized antithesis of division, hate, greed, violence, and scarcity.

Here is what I imagine: I imagine diocesan-sponsored peace academies in every diocese. I imagine diocesan-promoted intentional neighborhoods of black and white and brown. I imagine Catholic construction companies that as part of their charter only build houses for integrated and/or low-income or low-consuming (simple lifestyle) communities out of local materials with conservation and simplicity as their building priorities. I imagine peacemaking high schools—magnet Catholic high schools for those interested in studying Catholic social teaching, peacemaking strategies, and liberating lifestyles. I imagine designated prayer houses in those neighborhoods where violence is greatest, so that all people across the city can have a presence and pray for a new possibility, and so that they can work for what they pray. I imagine annual peacemaking awards in every parish and in every diocese, and that the event is the biggest banquet on the church calendar. I imagine parish picnics that are open to all and free to the poor. I imagine institutes that invite and train would-be or veteran politicians in the ways and needs of peace and justice. I imagine churches encouraging bicycling—lots of racks, with opportunities to turn in our cars (and our guns) for a new way of living. I imagine conflict resolution and Catholic social teaching and the study of justice as *core* courses in every Catholic grade school, high school, and college, including Notre Dame. I imagine green companies being started in every diocese with funding from the United States Conference of Catholic Bishops. I imagine the repopulation of farming communities with the financial support of parish communities in the city, which the farmers can then serve in a personal and direct way. I imagine, in an era of privately owned and run prisons, that the Catholic Church would buy and run a prison, to demonstrate what it means to try to love and help restore those who are inside. I imagine a church filled with peacemakers and prophets, where seeking justice, making peace, loving the broken, and dreaming a new dream for the world is our primary prayer: thy kingdom come.

The pursuit of peace in a culture of violence involves the creation of a new culture. I think this is *the* work of the parish.

8

Moving Parish to Mission

A Tool for the Task

The history of innovation is filled with "cross-pollinations," in which insights come by applying the rules or the work of one genre of human activity or knowledge to another.

While I was working at a Catholic parish in the 1980s and '90s, I crafted a program called JustFaith, which was a formation tool intended to introduce Catholic social mission to participants. It was, to my delight, profoundly impactful. By the force of its impact, it became a national program promoted by Catholic Charities USA, Catholic Campaign for Human Development, and Catholic Relief Services. (For the longer version of this story, see chapter 9.)

As the program grew, necessary changes occurred. JustFaith became JustFaith Ministries, a nonprofit organization with articles of incorporation, a budget, a board, and a mission statement. I had to change, too. I went from being an educator to becoming an executive director of a national organization. I am here to tell you, they are not the same.

As JustFaith Ministries grew and my responsibilities evolved, I tried to take whatever opportunities came my way to educate myself as an educator-turned-administrator. One experience that I am particularly thankful for was the invitation from a foundation to spend a week at Harvard University in a strategic thinking program. During this program I was introduced to the "logic model."

The logic model is a tool that helps nonprofit organizations design, evaluate, and communicate their work. Just about every high-functioning nonprofit uses some version of the logic model. It is critical for communicating with and inviting funders (foundations and private donors); it is necessary for evaluating the success or failure of the organization's activities; and it holds the organization together by insisting that it be mission-driven. In short, this is a critical tool for nonprofit work. Many, many nonprofits close each year, often because they failed to take seriously the responsibilities implied or assumed by the logic model.

Let me translate this importance briefly in the form of a quick (and contrived) conversation:

> Mike: Hi, John. Say, could I ask you to support our work with a donation?
>
> John: Perhaps. What does your organization do?
>
> Mike: We work with those who are homeless. You care about the homeless, don't you?
>
> John: Well, yes, I do care.
>
> Mike: Good. Then you'll give us a donation?
>
> John: Well, I don't think I know enough to make that commitment.
>
> Mike: What else do you need to know? You know me. You love Jesus. And Jesus cares about the poor.
>
> John: Could I ask a few questions?
>
> Mike: Of course!
>
> John: So, what do you actually do on behalf of those who are homeless? How has your work benefitted those

who are homeless? Are fewer people homeless because of your work? Do you have data about outcomes that I can look over? What is your budget? How is it spent?

Mike: John, these are a lot of complicated questions. We are an organization that has a simple love for the poor. Isn't that enough for you? Don't you trust us?

John: I do appreciate your good intentions, but if you want my money I need some assurances that my gift will have real impact.

In this very abbreviated conversation, what becomes clear is that for a nonprofit to thrive and inspire support, it needs to carefully plot, measure, demonstrate, and communicate effectiveness. Generous and skilled donors like John are not going to support good intentions, caring sentiment, or a heart full of love.

What follows is a more detailed, step-by-step description of how the logic model works. But let me first explain why a church community should be interested.

First, as I have traveled the country visiting parish after parish, the most common narrative is that they're losing members, especially young members. And while many people have opined as to why, the truth is that we really don't know why. Rarely do parishes and churches formally evaluate their work, their programs, their worship, their effectiveness, their staff, or their leadership. In truth, they don't know how to evaluate their work, because this was never understood to be important or even possible. That must change.

Second, as Pope Francis makes the case for a mission-oriented parish, suddenly the most important concept of nonprofit organizations, namely mission, is now also the most important concept in parishes. As described in previous chapters, Francis's emphasis on mission really has the power to radically remake parish self-understanding. The application of the logic model as a tool for parishes (think "new wineskins for new wine") insists that mission is the parish's primary function and presses important questions that most parishes don't typically navigate. The application of this tool gives us a way of evaluating where we might make some important changes that would enhance parish vitality and fidelity.

So, back to the logic model. How does it work?

Below is a diagram that depicts the "logic" of the process in a nonprofit organization's life:

Inputs → Activities → Outputs → Outcomes → Impact

Since the arrows flow from left to right, let's start from the left. I first describe these as they apply to a traditional nonprofit organization. Because these descriptions are a bit dry—and you might be tempted to skip over them—I want to encourage you to read these next few paragraphs carefully because they provide the foundation for a rather startling and revolutionary analysis of parish life as it has been and as it could be.

First, *inputs* simply refers to the assets that a nonprofit organization has to work with: everything from cash in the bank to physical facility to staff. Taking careful stock of what one has, expects to have, or needs to have in the way of resources helps an organization scale its expectations and think strategically about what can and can't be accomplished in the coming year(s). Of course, as an organization changes (grows or declines), the assets change. For this reason, it is important to evaluate regularly, probably annually, what the inputs (real and anticipated) are for the coming budgetary/operating cycle. As an example, a small, local nonprofit that runs a homeless shelter would list its inputs as savings in the bank, anticipated revenue (donations), the state of its building (any anticipated repairs?), and its volunteer corps, to mention just a few of the most obvious assets.

After considering the organization's inputs or assets, the second piece of the logic model is described as *activities*. Succinctly, activities are what an organization does with its assets or inputs. The activities are the services or planned efforts that an organization does in the name of its mission. So, in the case of the nonprofit running a homeless shelter, its primary activity is the work involved with providing shelter. The activities include the preparation of the space, the recruitment of volunteers, safety considerations, and possibly the communication with other service providers in preparation for possible medical emergencies. In short, activities are what an organization does with its collective time, energy, and resources.

Let me also mention that while the diagram above seems to depict a linear, one-direction relationship among the various components, in fact all the components interface dynamically with each other. For example, let's pretend that there is a critical need for the organization to enhance its work (activities) by hiring an operations manager (inputs). As you can see, in this case the influence is from right to left (activities to inputs), and then, as the operations manager goes to work, back to the right. The critical part of the logic model is that, when all the planning pieces are finally put together, there is a logical flow from left to right that provides a framework by which to understand and evaluate the organization's work.

The third component of the logic model process is called *outputs*. This refers to engagement; that is, when an organization offers a program (activity), how many people are served (outputs)? For example, in the case of the homeless shelter, how many people take advantage of the service that the shelter offers each night or in the course of an entire year? How does this number compare to previous years? Are there more children than last month? By measuring outputs, an organization can begin to evaluate the effectiveness of its work. It's not the only metric by which to judge effectiveness, but it is significant.

The fourth step in the process is called *outcomes*. This refers to what happened to those who participated ("outputs") in the organization's programs ("activities"). This fourth step has increased importance and complexity. While all the steps in the logic model are significant, they are ultimately tied to the climax of the fourth and fifth steps; nonprofits exist to make a change, address a problem, or deliver some kind of social good. If, for example, you are a part of a campaign to end cigarette smoking and your organization provides a lot of public service announcements (activities) that a lot of people see (outputs), but it doesn't change the rate of cigarette smoking (outcomes), then the feedback from outcomes would tell you that you need to change something, and soon. But there is even more complexity. To return to our example of the homeless shelter, the step of outcomes prompts the question about what an organization is hoping for by offering a particular service. In other words, offering a homeless shelter is a reasonable project if one's intended outcome is to make sure that a portion of those who are homeless in a particular geographical area have a safe place to sleep. On the other hand, if the intended outcome is to reduce or eliminate homelessness, one might legitimately question if running a homeless shelter is the correct use of energy. When a nonprofit recognizes the importance of naming its intended outcomes, it gives focus and rigor to its work.

The fifth step of the logical model, *impact*, is the guide star of the entire process; it's the dream, the vision, the great hope. It is also the most difficult to evaluate, partly because it names a reality too large to measure readily. In many ways, it is very close to outcomes, but it's more ambitious in scope and scale. For example, the organization that seeks to reduce smoking might aim to reduce smoking among teenagers by 10 percent next year; with effort and focus, progress (or lack thereof) toward that outcome can be measured. Its desired impact, however, is larger. The impact that it truly seeks might be described as "enhanced public health," with the recognition that reducing cigarette smoking means fewer people with cancer, fewer people with emphysema, fewer people with heart disease, and by implication, fewer children growing up without a parent who died from cancer, emphysema, heart disease, and so on. In other words, there is a very large benefit, a great social good (impact) that is linked to but not exhausted by the outcome. Impact *can* be measured but not perfectly; the measurements are more difficult since many, many factors influence public health, to use our example. And most of the time, even the best outcomes address only part of the great impact they seek. "Enhanced public health" might also mean, for example, increased services for those suffering from a mental illness (outcome), but an organization focused on reducing cigarette use is not going to tackle that problem.

Nonprofits often fail because they pay no attention to the importance of naming what they want to try to accomplish (outcomes and impact). Nonprofits are, by design, meant to be mission-driven, and just about everything they do should be arranged and defined around the mission, which is expressed in outcomes and impact. Many nonprofits define success wrongly by overidentifying with the number of programs offered (activities) or the number of people served (outputs), without reference to what they were trying to accomplish. When you don't know where you're trying to go, it's hard to figure out if you're getting there!

So, there's the summary (or *a* summary—there are many versions of this tool, some that are pretty much the same and others that go in different directions).

Now here's where the cross-pollination begins! What I'd like to explore is what happens when we apply this tool, the logic model, to the nonprofit called the local parish or church. What does it mean to engage the parish in a process of strategic planning and evaluation?

Let's begin the process again—focused on the parish—but instead of beginning with inputs, we start where every nonprofit must start: *impact*. What are we hoping for, reaching for, working for? What great good in the world are we hoping to accomplish or restore? What is our guide star?

Here, right away, is the sixty-four-thousand-dollar question: *What is a parish trying to accomplish?* We might even ask, what is the Universal Church trying to accomplish? My guess is that if we were to ask thirty different Catholics that question, we might get thirty different answers. Perhaps, if we were to ask thirty different theologians or bishops the same question, we might get at least twenty different answers. This is typically not a question that gets asked.

My guess is that many of the answers would focus on "bringing people to Christ" or "helping people discover God in their lives" or "getting people to come to Church" or "participation in the sacraments" or some variation of membership in the faith community. I'm concerned that these answers fall short.

I suggest that, in this matter of what a parish hopes to accomplish, we Christians rely on the foundation of our tradition. Is it reasonable to appeal to the testimony of Jesus for our answer?

Here's my observation: there is a concept, a dream, a hope, a vision to which Jesus refers more than any other idea in the four Gospels. *One hundred and forty-two times*, Jesus refers to a possibility that he calls the "kingdom of God" or the "reign of God." If we were to take a pair of scissors and cut out all the words that Jesus is credited with speaking in the four Gospels and then compile them into a pamphlet that we entitled *The Sayings of Jesus*, the subtitle could reasonably be, *The Proclamation of the Reign of God*. When Jesus is talking, he is talking about the reign of God. When Jesus is acting, he is embodying the reign of God. When he refers to himself, it is as a portal into the reign of God.

In other words, what Jesus was clearly passionate about and what he longs for his disciples to be passionate about is this vision and possibility called the reign of God. He says that it is "at hand" (Mark 1:15), which means that it's a real option, a real possibility. I would argue that our guide star, our hope, our dream as a Christian people is the reign of God. The great impact we seek is a reality in which the love of God reigns over all.

That's all well and good, and probably a thousand books have been written that address the meaning, the theology, or spiritual insights related to the reign of God. Alternatively, what I would like to do is to translate this rich religious vision (impact) into a set of outcomes that are clear and measurable. In other words, what is the identifiable fruit of this tree, this reality, called the reign of God?

As we start, let me address two likely objections. First, I realize that this approach risks the misunderstanding that Jesus's vision is fully understandable by looking at measurable outcomes; it is not. I am not trying to exhaust the meaning of the reign of God by looking for signs of its presence; on the other hand, I am certainly interested in defining and searching for those signs. Outcomes are not irrelevant; it is important to look for the reliable clues that what we are seeking is coming to pass. Jesus himself makes a similar observation about how to distinguish between true and false prophets: "You shall know a tree by its fruit" (Matt. 7:20). To apply this idea to our subject, we shall know a parish tree by its fruit. Good fruit, good tree. Good fruit, good parish.

Second, as we apply the various categories of the logic model—inputs, activities, outputs, and outcomes—to parish realities, it might feel like an imposition of secular business categories applied to spiritual terrain that seems reductionist and/ or awkward, or at least not very poetic. I think the process of the cross-fertilization I mentioned at the start of this chapter almost necessarily means some friction and uncomfortableness as we try to make links. I would be interested, pending the usefulness of this application, in seeing some thoughtful editing of the language of the logic model for an even better fit. With these objections acknowledged, let's return to our task.

Let me suggest that there are two kinds of fruit, two kinds of outcomes, that are immediately identifiable as reliable indicators of and progress toward the great impact called the reign of God. These two outcomes are so closely tied together that they cannot be described apart from each other.

The first outcome is the human person transformed. The language of transformation, *metanoia*, new sight, new life, rebirth, and redemption all speak to the human person made holy, made whole. For our purposes, let me suggest that we think of it this way: "Christ-likeness." Isn't it fair to suggest that one of the primary aims of Christianity is to invite believers into a spiritual journey that seeks, as its end, Christ-likeness? We are called to be Christ-like, to put on the "mind of Christ." And the characteristics of such—we'll call them outcomes—are mercy, compassion, love for the poor and vulnerable, hope, prayerfulness, and forgiveness, a list that is by no means exhaustive.

The second outcome, so intimately tied to the first, is the world transformed. The language of social transformation is articulated in the language of Catholic social teaching: justice, peace, inclusivity, restoration, community, solidarity, and an absence of deprivation, including no children starving, no children homeless, no children dying from preventable disease, no children dying from stray bullets or the bombs of war.

The obvious linkage between these two outcomes makes it difficult to talk about one without the other. In other words, if the first outcome happens (the human person transformed), the second (the world transformed) will naturally follow. In fact, if the second outcome does not happen, then that is evidence that the first outcome did not really happen (see chapter 9) or at least has not yet come to fruition. For example, if a person claims to be "saved by Christ" (personal transformation) but there's no evidence in his life of care of the poor or vulnerable, then the claim of personal transformation is suspect, since one of the fundamental fruits of faith is compassion (Matt. 5:25–41).

Let me make this plain: The compelling evidence that a parish or church is doing its work well is the transformation of the human person unto wholeness and the transformation of society unto wholeness. Everything Church must pay close attention to those two intertwined outcomes. Everything Church should model itself after the ministry of Jesus, which was to draw people into a transformational journey that would change them and impact the life of the world for the good. I think this is a good reiteration of Pope Francis's insistence that that the parish become "completely mission-oriented."

I'm aware that not all people of faith or leaders or theologians will agree with my position that the reign of God is the mission of the Church. Fine. I'm glad to be challenged. However, if it's not the reign of God, then what is it? In other words, it's fine to disagree, but the mission will still need to be defined, if not for the purposes of the logic model, then for the necessary effort to honor Pope Francis's beckoning for a missional Church, a church of mercy. Of course, the definition of the mission cannot be arbitrary and will have to pass theological and scriptural muster.

With that said our diagram—adapted for parish life—might look like this:

Inputs →	Activities →	Outputs →	Outcomes →	Impact
			Changed people	Reign
			and changed world	of God

With the parish mission (outcomes and impact) defined—changing people and changing the world—let's now start to the very left of the diagram and quickly consider the terms in the life of the parish.

First, when we apply the category of inputs to the reality of parish, we are considering the resources a local community of faith might have to work with. The obvious and typical ones are property, a set of buildings, staff, a weekly collection, and savings. We should also include a history, a long tradition, a sacred text, a sacramental tradition, a memory of holy witnesses, a linkage locally (diocese) and globally (universal church). And we must not forget the community, the people, the registered members.

Like any good organization, the parish or church might want to consider what resources it has that makes it distinctive—location, ethnicity, local history, and so on. By considering all of these assets, the frame of what a parish might seek to do in the next year or two—its impact—begins to take shape.

Here's the critical insight that the logic model offers: the assets of the parish are meant to serve the parish's mission. The purpose of parish resources is to be at the service of bringing people into a communion with God that yields personal and social wholeness.

For example, when a parish decides that it would like to do a building renovation or upgrade, it might ask itself not just what looks good but what will enable the transformation of its faith community and the transformation of its neighborhood or city. What resources should be committed to mission? What resources should go to building a literacy center for resettled refugees? What resources should go to providing education for low-income children? What resources should go to transitional housing? I am reminded of Salvadoran archbishop Oscar Romero, who refused to complete the construction of the new cathedral in San Salvador, insisting that only when the war in his country had ceased, and the hungry had been fed, and the children provided education, would he resume the project. In other words, the missional projects of peace, justice, and love were more important than buildings. However, assuming that building renovation needs to happen, the opportunity to think about mission-driven decision-making allows for a lot of fresh thinking about the physical campus.

Similarly, regarding staff resources, a parish might ask itself if the budget will or should allow for a staff position or two dedicated to the work of social change, empowering the parish to be effectively engaged in the healing of the wounds of poverty and abandonment. Dedicated budgeting for staff is a reliable sign of seriousness about the priorities of the parish. My experience is that a staff person dedicated to social mission, for example, typically translates into both significant social mission activity and significant parish vitality.

To summarize, the parish assets or inputs are meant for one thing and one thing only: to serve the parish's mission of transforming lives and transforming the local and global community.

The logic model stresses the importance of evaluation. Parish leadership—pastor, staff, and parish councils—will want to evaluate if their use of money, property, and staff is moving the community toward their missional goals: the reign of God—that is, transformed, holy people and a transformed, just society.

Second, what are the activities of the typical parish? To link with our previous discussion, activities are how the inputs of the parish are used. These include any of the offerings usually described in the Sunday bulletin: adult and youth education, Bible studies, sacramental preparation, sacramental celebrations, recreation, prayer opportunities, special events like retreats or guest speakers, opportunities to volunteer, and fundraising, such as parish dinners or festivals. The list is often very long. As discussed in chapter 3, however, the list, as long as it is, often neglects mission.

Let me emphasize again that the activities of the parish, like its inputs, are meant to serve the parish's primary mission. The logic model offers the caution that we *not* think of activities as our final mission. The end game is not to offer the most Bible studies or the most liturgies in town. Activities are one of the necessary steps by which we try to invite outcomes and impact, but they are not, in and of themselves, the achievement of the parish's mission or raison d'être.

It is not uncommon for proud parishioners to point to their voluminous Sunday bulletin and point excitedly at the dozens and dozens of activities happening just in the next week. Make no mistake, this can be a very good thing. However, if those activities are not focused on mission and instead are a grab bag of uncoordinated gatherings with little or no connection to the gospel invitation to become a people of mercy and generosity, then such busyness can be an expression of distraction instead of spiritual potency.

As we consider the importance of evaluation, it is critical that parish leadership take seriously the importance of evaluating all parish activities for their effectiveness in moving the parish toward its missional goals. It's doubly important that the Sunday liturgy—like all activities—be evaluated. If the preaching is mediocre, if the readers are untrained, if the music is uninspiring, if the experience is not engaging, then the liturgy will not transform. If fewer and fewer people are coming to Mass, a strategic evaluation allows inquiry and possible insight: What about the liturgy is so resistible? It seems to me it has been much too facile for church leadership to critique the culture as the reason for the decline in church attendance instead of considering whether the Sunday gathering is a compelling experience and what ingredients (might) make it more compelling.

Third, what are the outputs? Remember that outputs are simply the measure of who is participating in the activities that a parish is offering. So, outputs in most of today's parishes would include who and how many are coming to Mass, to youth ministry, and to Bible studies, to name a few. Consideration of outputs would ideally include comparisons with previous years: Is participation going up or down? What age groups participate? What programs are popular? Which ones are not? Why?

Outputs are a pressing consideration in many churches, since most churches are seeing a decline of one kind or another, especially among young people. Obviously, outputs are critical; there's not much accomplished by offering well-crafted programs and activities that no one is attending.

Outputs offer us the opportunity to look backwards and evaluate our programs. This evaluation might be divided into two categories: First, does participation tell us anything about the programs we are offering? Second, does participation tell us anything about the programs we are *not* offering? My hunch is that the decline of young people (ages nineteen to forty) in churches has more to do with the absence of life-changing experiences than a lack of interest in religion. Look at your parish bulletin and ask yourself if you are offering anything that would stir the heart and mind of the average young adult.

Fourth, we arrive back at outcomes. As the category of outcomes follows outputs, we must ask ourselves if we are getting the results we seek. In other words, when people participate in our offerings, do we see the kinds of change and growth or results we desired? If, in the name of the reign of God, we would hope to see our parish—each member—become more and more merciful, what does mercy look like? Trying to describe what mercy looks like might strike the reader as odd or impossible, but it's quite doable. Mercy looks like people making the effort to be engaged in the lives of those who are struggling or suffering somehow. A parish that wants to know if its members are becoming more merciful would endeavor to measure how many people are involved in the ministries of mercy this year compared to last year. It's true that someone volunteering at the soup kitchen is not infallible evidence of personal transformation, but it *is* a possible indicator of Christ-likeness. At the very least, it's a good sign—not infallible but a good sign nevertheless. To do a more careful consideration of personal transformation, it would be important for parish staff to listen to the testimonies of those working at the soup kitchen to hear their stories and to consider how the experience has changed them, or not.

Notice, for a moment, that mercy, expressed as care for those who are hungry at the soup kitchen, will only happen if the parish is encouraging such to happen. In other words, this is where the logic model helps us to strategize. If a parish commits staff time (inputs) to promote and organize volunteer options (activities) and puts together "soup kitchen teams" (outputs), then and only then can something like genuine mercy (outcomes) more likely happen. And this is just the start. As a parish gets more and more invested and interested in the work of the soup kitchen, it is quite likely to explore with more rigor and sophistication the issues of local hunger. The parish social ministry staff might be encouraged to begin to provide educational opportunities related to hunger that look into, for example, the problem of educating children who come to school hungry. The "mustard seed" of a soup kitchen team could grow into a robust commitment to address the causes as well as the symptoms of domestic poverty in the area.

And scenarios like these flower into our fifth and final category: Impact—the reign of God. What other name do we give to a reality in which generosity flowers and then ushers into commitment and investment, in which the poor and the rich encounter each other and sup together, in which the bonds of poverty are being addressed, in which the shackles of indifference are being released, in which lives are transformed by receiving food and by providing food, and through which church is made lively and lifegiving. No, it's not the reign of God in all its fullness, but it's a piece of it.

So let me offer a very specific—albeit abbreviated—example of how this model might play itself out in a parish; I include logic model labels as we go. Let's presume we're part of a somewhat stable, middle-class parish with about six hundred households, and one of the newly hired staff members, using the logic model, comes to a staff meeting with a new idea.

The staff member (*input*)—we'll call him "John"—observes that the parish is the closest church to the state prison. While some members of the parish have never thought of this as an asset, John sees it as an opportunity to fulfill Matthew 25 and "visit the prisoner." (Notice that what John has done here is to consider the parish *inputs*, which in this case include the Scripture tradition, a legacy of prison ministry, and the parish's location near a prison.)

John would like to start a prison ministry (*activity*). As soon as he says this, one of the older staff members groans out loud, "We've tried that. Two people visit the prison. That's all we've ever had." But John is not dissuaded. He mentions that the prison chaplain told him that they could use sixty more volunteers.

One of the other staff members tries to end the conversation by encouraging John to put something in the bulletin, where all parish dreams go to die an early death. John has other ideas.

John proceeds to share an idea that he thinks could successfully recruit and engage sixty parishioners. Here's the plan: he wants to invite Sr. Helen Prejean, author of *Dead Man Walking*, to speak about her experience working with prisoners (*activity*). He happens to know that she is a very good speaker and that, wherever she speaks, people take an interest in prison ministry. He would like this to happen in six months. Notice at this moment, John is talking about an *activity* (hosting a speaking event), but he is also talking about an *activity* that has a track record of *outcomes*. (Note: There is *no* reason for a parish to have an activity unless it is linked to an intended outcome.)

The first objection that John hears is that people in the parish are busy and only a small number of people will attend (*output*), but John was expecting that objection and has a plan. John shares that he would like for the staff to go through the parish roster and identify the sixty people in the parish who might be most interested in hearing Sr. Helen, and after identifying them, ask them to attend a special gathering hosted by the pastor and staff next month. Each of the sixty are to receive a personal call from the staff inviting them to a meeting to explain the project. Who are the sixty? They are the folks who are known to have some interest in social action or in the work at the prison or who have been generous with their time in other projects. They are to be invited to commit themselves to come to a wine-and-cheese gathering next month. Of course, some will have to or want to decline; in that case, the staff will go back to the parish roster and find replacements. The staff will continue to call or meet with people one on one until sixty people commit to the meeting. This part of the plan is based upon the proven results of personally inviting people one on one, an activity that *always* yields increased outputs.

John explains that, at the meeting, he, the pastor, and the staff will present their plan: they will share their gospel interest to address the many, many needs that exist at the prison; the abandonment and suffering of prisoners is well-documented. In addition, the experience of those who participate in prison ministry is that it deepens their faith (outcome) and provides profoundly important experiences of walking in the footsteps of Christ (outcome). As is often the case, those who get involved in a ministry like this find themselves more committed to their parish (outcome). John shares that the parish would like to start a prison ministry (activity) and that the parish is committed to investing resources (input) into the education, training, and spiritual reflection (activity) of those involved. John wants to engage the sixty with the plan and the vision and then conclude with a personal request that all sixty of those present commit themselves (output) to attending Sr. Helen's presentation.

John then continued: With 60 people already committed to attending, the plan is to also invite the rest of the parish using pulpit announcements, bulletin invitations, and a letter from the pastor. Other churches in the area will also be invited. John hopes that as many as 100 to 150 people attend. This, by the parish's standards, would be a very good response (output).

So, the anticipation is that Sr. Helen will come in six months and give her presentation (activity) in front of 100-plus people (output), who are delighted, impressed, and inspired (notice the benefit of recruiting well) to see so many of their fellow parishioners in attendance. After Sr. Helen is done, and after the enthusiastic applause, the pastor will then take the microphone and announce to all those in attendance that the parish is taking Sr.

Helen's work seriously and would like to ask every person in attendance to return in two months for an already-planned all-day training for those getting started in prison ministry (activity), offered in collaboration with the diocese and an organization that specializes in such training. The pastor pleads for everyone to "give it a try" (output), even if they're not sure this is something they know they want to do. (Notice that the purpose of Sr. Helen's talk is not entertainment. It's not just to have a big event. It is part of a strategy of engagement.)

Two months later, the training is offered (activity). Eighty-five people show up, sixty-five of them from the parish (output). To everyone's delight, a few months later, a prison ministry is hatched with over fifty people participating (outcome). It's a staggering response to a well-crafted, well-strategized project. Along the way, it took a lot of work, navigating the parish's inputs, strategizing activities, working hard for outputs, and all the while aiming for outcomes. And, yes, it takes a lot of effort. And, yes, it's *very* satisfying to see the fruit of hard work come to bear. John is a very happy man.

Final chapter of this story of hope: Three years later, inspired by their work at the prison and the relationships that have developed, those involved in the parish's prison ministry helped fund a new parish project: a temporary residence for those finishing their prison sentence to help them with the transition. The new project inspires a whole new group of people, including some young adults, to get involved. Along the way, some of the business owners in the parish take an interest and offer job training and jobs to some of those in transition. In time, those who once were prisoners at a distance are now friends in the community. Some even join the parish; it is, after all, the place where their people are, the people who brought hope.

What's your parish's dream?

9

Formation unto Transformation

The Story of JustFaith

In 1988 I was hired by Church of the Epiphany in Louisville, Kentucky, for the position of minister of social responsibility, which included oversight of the work of outreach and social action.

Church of the Epiphany was a parish that had a lot going for it: a beautiful campus, a large staff, an energetic pastor, wonderful liturgies, and a deep commitment to lay engagement. It is located in a wealthy part of Louisville, so it's no surprise that it had an ample budget. What *is* a surprise was that it had chosen to allocate part of its budget to a full-time position dedicated to the work of social ministry. Very few parishes, even those with lots of resources, make that commitment. I applied and was hired.

I had learned during the interview process that, while the pastor and some members of the parish were quite committed to social mission, the vast majority of members were not. My job, in part, was to widen the net.

I had spent the previous six years in Colorado Springs and for the last five of those years was a member of a Catholic Worker community,[1] working primarily with homeless men and women. I was well aware from that experience that most parishes were not very engaged in social mission. In fact, in the cover letter of my application for the job, I had written, "I realize that social ministry will only involve a small number of people, that it will happen mostly on the periphery of parish life, and that it will be eyed suspiciously by most of the rest of the parishioners. Knowing this as I do is probably an asset." The truth is, I wasn't expecting a lot.

For the first year of the job, all my expectations were met: not much happened. It seemed like no matter what I planned or organized, I could anticipate that about eight people would show up. And it was always the *same* eight people. In a parish with twelve hundred households, this was discouraging at best.

I admit that the transition from the Catholic Worker to the parish was more of a shock than I had anticipated it would be. My wife and I had left a small intentional community, modeled after the Catholic Worker, in which every one of the members was passionate about justice, peacemaking, and hospitality for the poor and marginalized, and come to a very large community where little of this passion was in evidence. It was spiritually disorienting. Was it really possible to be a Catholic church and not care about the world's wounds? Apparently so.

It was tempting to self-righteously "stomp the dust off my feet" and quit, except for one thing: most of the people in the parish were perfectly likeable. They loved their kids, a great many of them were obviously committed to the parish, and they volunteered generously for a variety of projects. They were thoughtful

---

[1] I use the phrase "Catholic Worker community" for ease of description. Since the composition of the community was a combination of Catholics and Mennonites, it was decided not to use that description. However, the community modeled itself very closely after the Catholic Worker format.

and kind to me, even if almost none of them ever attended anything I tried to offer.

And in this odd mix of human warmth and professional failure, the answer dawned on me one day. Obviously, these were not mean-spirited, uncaring, unfeeling people. These were ordinary people who were just unfamiliar with an important part of their own tradition, called Catholic social teaching. And why were they unfamiliar? Could it have been because there had not been a single opportunity in their lives as Catholics to become familiar with it? I realized at that moment that it was the lack of opportunity, not malice or indifference, that was at the root of their disengagement. And, in that instant, I went from judgment and condemnation to recognizing myself. Had it not been for the remarkable opportunity to study theology in college and grad school and to accidentally bump into the Catholic Worker, I am quite sure I never would have found my way to social mission on my own. I was who I was because a lot of people had taught and mentored me.

And this got me thinking: How might I re-create for adults in the parish the opportunity I had in school and in the Catholic Worker? Obviously, most people can't quit their jobs and take a sabbatical from their families to pursue a degree in theology or join an intentional community. What kind of parish-friendly process or program could have a similar impact?

I could only think of one.

Over the span of five years I had previously served as the director of the Rite of Christian Initiation for Adults (RCIA) at three different parishes. I was repeatedly struck by the obvious transformation for many, many people that would occur during the process. One of the most obvious examples of change included some of those who came into the RCIA quite reluctantly, perhaps because they were accommodating their fiancée or spouse and not particularly interested in church. It was not uncommon over the course of eight to twelve months to see an obvious metamorphosis that was celebrated at Easter and resulted in committed and impassioned new Catholics who almost immediately made an energetic investment in parish life. Many of them later became leaders of the parish.

Reflecting on the RCIA, there are several ingredients that made/make it so potentially impactful. First, like getting a graduate degree, it is *long*—not as long as a master's program, of course, but long by any standard of parish life. The length of the process is critical because it provides an appropriate amount of time for something substantial to happen. Most change, conversion, growth, or transformation (all synonyms) takes time. Most people don't change easily or quickly. The length of the RCIA allows time for people to integrate the message; it allows time for a lot of conversation and prayer and teaching to happen. The length just honors the terms of a substantial *metanoia*. To say this another way, a long process gives the Holy Spirit a lot of room to work.

Second, the RCIA offers a learning process that, for the purposes of transformation, is superior to getting an academic degree in theology. The weaving together of prayer, retreat, Scripture, teaching, conversation, and community building means that learning is being integrated in all kinds of ways: intellectual, emotional, spiritual, and relational. This kind of networked and multifaceted integration is the key to an effective formation process.

Third, in the RCIA processes that I oversaw we read good books, invited compelling speakers, watched stimulating videos, shared in carefully crafted prayers, and took powerful retreats. Participants and their sponsors were afforded a rather substantive introduction and exploration of the theological and spiritual traditions of the church. My experience is that the more theological content and spiritual sophistication people get, the more they want, the more they invest of themselves. We were forming real spiritual seekers. Frankly, it was hard to finish the process unchanged! The RCIA was really the first widely available substantive formation process for Catholic lay adults. Prior to the RCIA, most Catholic adults had to rely on their memory of the *Baltimore Catechism* they learned as children for their theological education.

Fourth, while the RCIA is fundamentally a process of faith formation, learning, and growth, it happens in the catalyzing medium of community. People grow and learn differently in relationship. This makes a process like the RCIA even more potent than, say, an academic class where people listen to lectures, even excellent lectures. Moreover, people who start the RCIA together as strangers routinely become friends and can then anticipate an ongoing relationship as fellow parishioners. Classmates at a university might also build friendships, which typically have an expiration date called graduation, after which people often scatter across the country. The RCIA, in effect, begins a lot of long, local friendships anchored in conviction and hope and geography.

These four ingredients speak to the critical linkage between formation and transformation. A robust, thoughtful formation process does not guarantee transformation, but it does provide the heightened possibility, even the likelihood, that transformation can happen. You can't put the Holy Spirit in a box with a bow, but it is the Church's experience that certain kinds of formation often yield powerful results.

Back to the story: I decided to craft a formation process that would take advantage of these ingredients of the RCIA, but instead of preparing participants for membership in the Catholic Church, this process was intended to prepare people for social mission. I was hoping this adaptation, which I would call "JustFaith," would have the effect of making people passionate about the work of mercy and justice.

What did the adaptation look like? The first iteration of JustFaith at Church of the Epiphany was thirty-six weekly sessions (early September to late May). Each session, which I typically scheduled for Tuesday evening, was two and a half hours long. In addition, there were three retreats near the beginning, middle, and end of the program. These were held off-site at a retreat center and lasted from Friday evening through Sunday noon. In addition, there were special events that we would add to the calendar: educational offerings from the Peace & Justice Office of the Archdiocese of Louisville (which no longer exists), events sponsored by one of the many justice-oriented organizations in town, and others.

Everything in the process—prayers, books, videos, guest speakers, retreats, and special events—was focused on some aspect of social mission: the scriptural and theological foundations, the voices of the poor, testimonies of saints, prophets and holy people, church documents, the work of Catholic social action agencies, social analysis, and the spirituality that integrated the values of compassion, mercy, and justice.

I initially advertised to the parish with a flier that described the program's various components and invited people to consider the process with a series of questions: Are you interested in exploring a piece of our tradition that has not received a lot of attention? Are you interested in looking at the scriptural foundations of mercy and justice? Are you interested in exploring the intersection of spirituality and action? And so on. The very last question read, "Are you open to the possibility that your life might change?" I included this question because of the memory of what had happened to catechumens in the RCIA.

Twelve people signed up that first year. Sometimes people ask me, "How did you get twelve people to sign up for a nine-month program when you had trouble getting ten to come to a single meeting?" I attribute their interest to that last question: "Are you open to the possibility that your life might change?" Having been involved with JustFaith locally and/or nationally for most of the last twenty-five years, what I know now is that a lot of people in parishes are looking for a fresh possibility for their lives. They are looking for something that will fill their hearts and spirit. They are looking for something that will ask a lot of them. They may come to church Sunday after Sunday, but they return to their lives wondering if climbing ladders or collecting stuff or staring at TV, computer screens, and cellphones is the crescendo of life. The gospel offers all of us an alternative!

So, the thirteen of us got started. And here's what happened: everybody changed! It happened slowly for some and shockingly fast for others, but everybody changed. The early evidence of this change was the growing passion and excitement that built from week to week. People would talk about how they couldn't wait for the next session. After the weekly two-and-a-half-hour gathering, people would stick around and talk in our meeting room or the church parking lot for another hour. Folks would just say, almost weekly, "I can't believe how much this means to me!"

The best evidence of the changes that happened is simply the descriptions of what people did after the program was over. Back in 1996 I wrote an article for *Salt of the Earth* magazine in which I described some of the changes that had happened to participants between 1989 and 1996; here is an edited excerpt:

> Pat B. left an engineering job with a major corporation out of concern for the dehumanization he experienced in the workplace and an interest in nurturing young people; he now teaches at a Catholic high school.
>
> Spouses Gary and Mary B. went through the program together. Mary went on to become the chairperson of Louisville's Council on Peacemaking, and she started

Louisville's only Pax Christi group. She also began her own business in socially responsible investing. Gary got involved with Prisoner Visitation Service, visiting federal inmates in Lexington. He also regularly works at a homeless shelter. Together, they have visited El Salvador and Haiti and they provided a sizable donation to start a micro-loan program in Haiti.

David H. oversaw the beginning of a sister-parish relationship with a community in El Salvador, which has prompted over fifty parishioners to visit this Third World country.

Martha D. is now on the local board of Habitat for Humanity and served as chairperson of the parish social-concerns committee. Rosetta F. spent three months in El Salvador and worked to create local markets for Salvadoran crafts. Chris B. began a parish committee trying to address issues of racism.

Mike O. was the chief financial officer for a major health-care provider; he grew weary of the overemphasis on profit and longed to do something that connected directly with his faith. Today he works in development for a residential facility for at-risk teenage boys.

Rosemary S., Mary Sue B., Jackie C., and Keiron O. began a women's concerns committee and were also responsible for a yearlong program on the role of women in the church, inviting such speakers as Mary Luke Tobin, Richard McBrien, and Catherine Hilkert, not to mention some outstanding local speakers.

David C. oversaw a yearlong discernment process on the matter of civil rights for homosexuals. Bob and Dotti L. have made at least eight trips to El Salvador, one lasting six months. Mike O. is also involved with a grassroots inner-city organization funded by the Campaign for Human Development.

Other participants have gone on to be involved in parish social-action committees, legislative networks, material-aid collections, and so on. Many have simplified their lifestyles—everything from moving to less expensive homes to eating less meat to just buying less. And many have become very generous with their wealth.[2]

Of course, since 1996 many more changes have happened to the people described above, and many, many more people have gone through the program and made new choices of their own. I have fifty pages of conversion stories I could tell, stories of remarkable and even heroic commitments.

What was particularly exciting to me was not just the changes to individuals but changes to the parish. Each year that JustFaith was offered, a new group of fired-up parishioners would exit the program ready to set the world ablaze. At a certain point— I believe it was after the fourth year of offering the program—there was a kind of shift in the parish. With over fifty JustFaith graduates energetically involved in starting new social action subcommittees, initiating new projects, sharing their newfound voice on parish council, teaching third-grade catechesis, and just generally creating a very big swirl of social action activity, the parish seemed to come alive with a fresh energy. New people started joining the parish because of its public witness and growing reputation as an "activist parish." Liturgies, as an expression of the community's breadth of commitments, came alive with the linkage between Eucharist and an active love. Yes, there was pushback by some members; some left the parish. Retrospectively, I realize I made some mistakes

[2]   From "How to Turn a Lukewarm Parish into a Hotbed of Social Justice," *Salt of the Earth* magazine, September/October 1996.

amid all this activity and wish I had been more attentive to those who were uncomfortable with the changes that were happening. On the other hand, I would guess that for every person who left to find another parish, five took their place. It was not uncommon for the Sunday liturgies to have standing room only. This was one rockin' place.

It was a great time to be Church. Our pastor (Joe Graffis) was wonderfully supportive; the archbishop (Thomas Kelly) was appreciative.[3] The work of compassion, mercy, and justice flowered. It was, in fact, the single most powerful parish renewal I have ever witnessed or read about in the North American Church. Interestingly, it was never intended to be a renewal or even called that. Nevertheless, I think what Pope Francis was hoping for in 2017 (see chapters 1 and 2) was glimpsed about twenty-five years ago at a parish in Louisville, Kentucky.

It wasn't long before word got out about what was happening. People started to hear about this program called JustFaith. I was asked to write a couple of articles that were printed in national journals, and suddenly I was being contacted for the program syllabus and to give talks on the program. To make a long story short, this all culminated with an opportunity to offer JustFaith nationally under the umbrella and banner of Catholic Charities USA, beginning in 2000. A new chapter of JustFaith was about to begin.

The first national version of JustFaith looked much like the original parish version. It was shortened from thirty-six sessions to thirty; retreats were lessened from three to two. However, it was decided to add extra emphasis on encounter, so four immersion experiences were built into the program. One of these experiences was the "Journey to Justice" experience that had been crafted by

---

[3] In 1995 I received the archdiocese's Peace and Justice Award, mostly because of the impact of JustFaith on the parish.

Catholic Campaign for Human Development to provide an opportunity for participants to witness the energy and power of low-income communities organizing for justice. Over the years, the JustFaith program has been repeatedly revised to respond to feedback from organizers and participants.

From 2000 to date, JustFaith has been offered all over the country with the support and partnership of a lot of nationally known organizations; at various times over the years, JustFaith Ministries has partnered with Catholic Charities USA; Catholic Relief Services; Catholic Campaign for Human Development; Pax Christi USA; Pax Christi International; the US Catholic Bishops' Office of Justice, Peace, and Human Development; Maryknoll; and Bread for the World. The program has been offered in over one hundred Catholic dioceses, in over fifteen hundred parishes, with more than fifty thousand participants.

The stories of transformation are vast. This is the reason our partners were more than glad to invest resources into our work: graduates of JustFaith get involved! They sign up to be organizers of Bread for the World's Offering of Letters. They become donors and board members for their local Catholic Charities. They organize Catholic Relief Services' Lenten Rice Bowl. They are participants in Maryknoll's immersion trips around the world. They advocate for the low-income communities funded by Catholic Campaign for Human Development. In addition, numerous nonprofits and nonpartners have benefitted significantly. Habitat for Humanity and St. Vincent de Paul, for example, have recruited hundreds of volunteers, board members, advocates, and donors from the ranks of JustFaith graduates. Moreover, dozens of Just-Faith grads changed careers and went to work for one of the organizations described above. Dozens and dozens of nonprofits have benefitted significantly from the passion and commitment that was birthed in those who went through the JustFaith process. In fact, some JustFaith graduates started nonprofits because of their passion for social mission, first awakened by JustFaith.

In parishes where the local bishop or at least the pastor was invested in social mission, JustFaith has sometimes been offered year after year for over ten years! You can imagine the impact of over one hundred JustFaith graduates engaged and organized in a parish. There are some exciting stories of parish renewal resulting from the embrace of JustFaith.

With that said, it must be observed that these renewals—as powerful as they are—need constant nurture. If a bishop or pastor is replaced with someone who is not invested in social mission and chooses to withdraw support, these renewals will mutate into something other than parish energy and enthusiasm. In my experience, instead of the parish being a beehive of faith in action, this energy will leave the campus and find its way to a lot of local and national nonprofits; this is not a bad thing, but it is a far cry from what was or could have been. If I am reading Pope Francis correctly, he would prefer that this energy for compassion be the heartbeat of the parish and the drumbeat of the mission of the parish to the world. I think this is the only formula for bringing young people to (or back to) the parish.

What does the JustFaith story mean? I think there are five lessons for those involved in formation and one caution for preachers.

First, *all formation must,* must, *include formation for compassion, outreach, and social mission.* The ultimate point of formation is not to convey a litany of creeds and theological formulas. The point of formation is forming a human being: forming a mind for love (the Mind of Christ), forming a heart for love (spirituality), and forming a life for love (discipleship). What Pope Francis calls a "missionary disciple" is really another phrase for a grateful reply to God's gift and a tender response to the world's cry. Here's the point:

If the formation ministries of the parish do not result in people caring for the poor and vulnerable, it's not acceptable. Period.

Second, *formation needs to include encounters off campus.* The tools of the trade certainly include maps like creeds and theological formulas, but these are just maps. So, for example, if we want to introduce Jesus's teaching on the Good Samaritan, it is important to read and reread the text, to introduce the "Corporal Works of Mercy," to introduce people to the witness of St. Vincent de Paul, and to highlight some of the hundreds of references in papal encyclicals. It is good to watch the movie *Romero*, and video material from Catholic Relief Services. All of these very good and important activities can be done conveniently on parish property. Even so, they are still quite incomplete. Before, during, or after this learning from a distance, there must be encounter, firsthand experience, direct contact, relationship. People are formed most powerfully by interacting with the real. Formation must stop being solely an on-campus activity focused primarily on theological concepts.

Third, formation should include options that are robust, substantial, and challenging. Jesus asked his disciples to drop whatever they were doing to follow him. Religious communities ask their members to make lifelong commitments to vows of obedience, chastity, and poverty. Mormons ask every one of their young people to take two years of their life to go door to door. Jesuit Volunteers give one or two years of their life to serve in poor places. Priests are asked to serve for a lifetime. Jewish children start studying Hebrew every week at a very young age. The parish inclination to offer only programs that are quick, easy, and light is a dead end. If we ask little, that is exactly what we'll get. For the record, I am not suggesting that we require lifetime or even yearlong commitments, but I think the parish should be the place that offers both shorter and longer offerings. My experience as a student studying theology and my experience as a full-time member of a Catholic

Worker community is that many people appreciate the possibility of making an investment into something big. The testimony of JustFaith is that people can and will make substantial commitments, especially if there is the prospect of a life-changing payoff. Most parishes, to date, have not offered that option.

Fourth, *formation is best done in the community.* The most powerful formation that I have known has been done side by side. One of my favorite memories during a JustFaith session was when one of the participants said, in response to something she had read that week, "Well, I can't keep living the way I've been living." And when she said this, every other participant in the room was suddenly forced to ask, *Then what does this mean for me?* In other words, when we learn together, we learn not only the common material that might be in a syllabus, but we learn *through* the others in the room. Each person becomes an incarnate vessel of faith wrestling with possibilities. Moreover, to the extent that our faith tradition sometimes asks very challenging questions, we need one another for the strength to move forward, to say yes, to affirm "amen." With the support and understanding of each other, most of us can do things we could never do on our own.

Fifth, *the richest formation experiences marry the inner and the outer.* Prayer and action are joined at the hip. Action, uninformed by deliberate spiritual practices, can soon become angry or cynical. Prayer, uninformed by the practice of love, can become narcissistic and far-flung. More important, prayer can often liberate generosity and resolve, just as action can open up spiritual insight and self-awareness that is otherwise unavailable. As a result, formation for compassion is not just a matter of studying the wounds of the world but also the wounds of the self. Similarly, to learn to love is not just about the dynamics of listening to and presence with one's children and friends but also about knowing what in the world needs loving—what the world looks like, for example, outside of my comfortable suburb. To become mature Christians is indeed about nurturing our sense of the presence of the holy, as it is known both in quiet as well as the rough-and-tumble of life. My hunch is that parishes should essentially be centers of social action and spiritual practice (and good potlucks to make it all that much more interactive).

Finally, let me address priests and deacons and anyone else who gives homilies or sermons. Do not presume your preaching, regardless how good it is, will be enough to engage people in social mission. Your preaching must be a part of a larger orientation within the parish or church that makes social mission a priority. I have known too many pastors with great hearts, a fine education in Catholic social teaching, and excellent homiletic skills who find themselves alienated from their parishioners because nothing else in the parish was preparing the congregation for what they would hear on Sunday morning. You will not preach your church into submission. Make sure people have lots of opportunities at your parish to study Catholic social teaching, read the lives of the saints, and learn about the great Catholic agencies. Plan lots of opportunities for people to cross the tracks and get involved in the lives of those who are poor and vulnerable. Arrange for lots of retreats that support and encourage social mission spirituality. Then—and maybe only then—will your sermons nourish and challenge.

The testimony of JustFaith is that there is something personally and communally transforming about engaging, educating, preparing, celebrating, and commissioning people for the work of mercy, compassion, and justice. This, I think, is a fair representation of what Jesus was about. The future of the Church will depend on how well we embrace this gospel invitation and make it the cornerstone of faith formation and, in fact, of all that we do in the parish.

10

Love and Pray

A Path to Spiritual Maturity

Matthew 25:31–46 ("I was hungry and you gave me food")—a Gospel text that shows up on the Feast of Christ the King, the last Sunday of the Catholic liturgical year—suggests that a critical touchstone and measure for the true disciple is the embrace of and care for all, evidenced by relationship with those who are typically "the excluded," namely the poor, the outcast, the stranger, the enemy, and the one who inconveniently presses upon my time, attention, and conscience. In Catholic social teaching, this moral and spiritual beckon is called the "preferential option for the poor and vulnerable."

In effect, the wisdom of Jesus describes the powerful, but often neglected, bridge between spiritual insight and social action/ real compassion. In fact, the wisdom of Jesus seems to suggest that the link is even more intimate than a bridge; it is the collapse of the two categories altogether. The separation of spirituality from action is a false one. In other words, we are not called to do spiritual practices—prayer, study, meditation, retreat, ritual—to "find God" and then make our way, now inspired, to the work of mercy and justice. In fact, it might be argued that, if anything, it's just the reverse: Love those who struggle with poverty and suffer abandonment, and the effect is that we will find ourselves on a path that

133

leads to insight, maturity, prayer, wisdom, and Christ-likeness. If, however, we choose to avoid engagement and community with those who suffer, we will certainly live an incomplete life, including an incomplete spiritual life.

To put it rightly, the practice of prayer and the practice of compassion are *both* necessary and complementary spiritual practices. We are called to be both activists and mystics, missionaries of love and contemplatives, great lovers and deep thinkers. And, in all of that, the spiritual journey can happen; in all of that, we can be made whole; in all of that, the world can be made whole. In other words, in the alternating rhythm of relationship and reflection, action and inaction, engagement and solitude, availability to the other and availability to silence, *becoming* can happen. The practice of prayer and the practice of compassion are activated by each other, like a chemical reaction. Hydrogen cannot make water by itself. Oxygen cannot make water by itself. Put them together, water happens, and life can flourish.

Over the last twenty years of extensive travel, going from parishes and churches to diocesan offices and social agencies, from lectures and retreats to one kind of church convening or another, constantly bumping into people of faith, I find myself repeatedly impressed by the centeredness, the appealing presence, the breadth of spirit, the great-heartedness, the wholeness, indeed the joy of those whom I know to be people of committed and determined compassion and prayer.

Since the Second Vatican Council, the vocabulary of spirituality has certainly enjoyed something of a flowering. A word that was never used and poorly understood by my Catholic parents is now a familiar piece of the Catholic/Christian/religious lexicon. The language of *spirituality* speaks to becoming, maturation, integration, personal awareness, and a felt sense of the sacred and holy.

So much could and should be said and celebrated about this vivification of such an important religious concept.

With that said, I offer the following observation with some trepidation that I will sound grouchy and self-righteous. An awful lot that describes itself as "Christian spirituality" is glaringly devoid of any sense of feeding the hungry, clothing the naked, or visiting those in prison. Much of Christian spirituality—indeed, much of what we call church or Christianity—seems sadly disengaged from the vision and message of Jesus and the embrace of an authentic and inclusive love—what Pope Francis calls "mercy."

To describe this in one succinct experience, several years ago Maggie and I attended a weekend conference focused on spirituality. Prior to the formal conference, there was a preconference event that highlighted the reflections of some folks who were working on human trafficking issues in Africa, which Maggie and I were grateful to attend. It was lightly attended, perhaps because it involved an extra day that people would have to take off from work. In any event, the speakers described and reflected on their work, which was nothing short of extraordinary and heroic, addressing almost unbearable human pain and crisis. Maggie and I were in awe. At the question-and-answer period, one middle-aged man asked, in a respectful, good-natured way, why this preconference event was offered, since this was a conference on spirituality. He humbly admitted he did not understand the connection.

My worry is that much of what passes for spirituality and spiritual practice—prayer days, meditation, retreats, spiritual direction, contemplation, ritual, and study—is primarily informed by an exclusive attention to the self and perhaps family relationships, suggesting that much of what we call "spirituality" is some mixture of psychology and private devotion, made sacred by the use of religious imagery (a *lot* of religious words). My argument is not that it's worthless but that it's woefully incomplete. I am concerned that it provides a very limited experience of what Jesus seems so passionate about, namely the reign of God, the most-repeated phrase in the four Gospels.

As I understand the reign of God, it includes the grace-driven, love-driven transformation of the self and the world; what's more, it recognizes that transformation of self and world are directly connected to each other. Many writers have made this point: "The state of the soul is the state of the social order." The world cannot be changed by love to become just unless *we* are changed by love to become whole, but we cannot be made whole without engaging in the work of making the world whole. Personal transformation and social transformation are one piece.

Isn't it instructive that the spiritual formation of the original disciples happens with Jesus on the road? In effect, the disciples grow by doing, and then discussing, and then praying, and in all kinds of mixtures of those three activities. They grow into an understanding of this God of love (1 John 4:8), this God of compassion (Matt. 25:31–47), this God who loves justice (Isa. 61:8), this God who makes all things new (Rev. 21:5), by participating as active observers and agents of love, compassion, justice, and newness. And, yes, necessarily, they pause with Jesus to reflect, ask sometimes stupid questions, and pray. But the spiritual adventure described in the four Gospels does not happen in the sanctuary; it happens mostly on the road, in the company of sinners, beggars, prostitutes, and lepers.

The spiritual life is perhaps best described by drawing from one of Pope Francis's favorite phrases; he insists that we're all called to be "missionary disciples," that is, people who deliberately place ourselves in the company of the world's wounds, seeking communion, healing, new possibilities, hope, and life. If this is true, then anything that describes itself as concerned with spirituality will necessarily be connected to geography. If we are to be attentive to the world's reality, with special attention to its suffering, we must position our bodies and hearts accordingly. As a matter of spiritual growth, we will eat, pray, and breathe in unexpected places.

I am reminded of conversations I've had over the years while serving on the residential staff at the University of Notre Dame and as a member of staff at wealthy parishes about "What is God calling me to do?" I'm very aware that when we are comfortable, fully satiated, and content, the question feels almost sterile. If we figuratively or literally get on our knees at the golf course and ask sincerely, "What is God calling me to do?" the answers to the question will seem fleeting, mysterious, or conjured. The only true answer—which probably will not avail itself—is "Spend less time at the golf course," or more accurately, "Spend more time in places where golf cannot even be imagined."

Juxtaposed with this memory is another memory of being in Oakland to do a presentation. While I was in town, I was invited by my host to participate in a solidarity walk through a neighborhood that had been wracked by a stretch of recent drive-by shootings. The Catholic bishop of Oakland, Michael Barber, was present, and our message was simply, "We are for you," "We share your grief," and "We will work together to bring an end to this pain." As we walked, it was hard not to notice that half of the homes were boarded up or in significant disrepair. Sidewalks were crumbling, roads had potholes, and little was green or cared for. This place was suffering from a lack of jobs, a lack of businesses, a lack of care, and lack of hope. In appearance, it looked a bit like a mixture of a ghost town and a war zone. And I thought to myself, if any one of us were to get on our knees and ask, "What is God calling me to do?" the answers would not have been mysterious at all (because the invitation was swirling around us even before we asked the question):

"Rebuild this place," "Help to heal this community," "Be a vessel of hope in what is around you."

There is little question that when we avail ourselves to what Jesus availed himself, our prayers can have ready answers. Jesus not only taught us *how* to pray, he taught us *where* to pray. If I frame my prayer as a matter of personal salvation and personal fulfillment, the prayer is unanswerable. If I frame my prayer as a matter of opening myself up to a love for the world, answers abound.

The true spiritual quest is not that you or I become whole. Rather, informed by the belief that the world is birthed by God and is precious and sacred and one, the true spiritual quest is that the world become whole—and you and I along with it.

11

Last Things

In the Introduction, I mentioned that there were five important personal experiences that informed the content of this book. There was actually a sixth.

In 2004 I was diagnosed with advanced cancer and given poor prospects for survival. At age forty-eight and with three children not out of high school, this was hard news to bear; like most people, I had not expected to die before I was fifty. In the turmoil of surgery, chemo, and the unknown, I started to navigate the prospect of dying soon. Some of it, I admit, was not navigable. It was nearly impossible to look at my daughters and think that I would not see any of them graduate, go to college, get their first job, marry, or have children of their own. On the other hand, I was aware that parents die young all the time and that their spouses and children survive and can even thrive over time. I was grateful for that consoling thought.

Anticipating that I had very little time, I started a tentative bucket list. I began by writing down exotic ideas like trips to Hawaii, a new truck (I'm sure my widowed wife would have loved having that after I was gone!), and so on. But after giving each item on my list deeper consideration, I came to the unexpected conclusion that I already "had" everything I could ask for, except maybe a few more years of life. I realized that I was full.

Specifically, what I happily and unexpectedly came to understand was that, even as it might be coming to an end, my life felt overflowing. No, I hadn't done everything I thought I might, I had not reached some state of perfect peace, and I had not said everything I needed to say to those I loved. But I was full. The fullness that I sensed was not something I had accomplished; it was something given. It was a sense of meaning and purpose understood and lived. Since I was a boy, the faith tradition that had been handed to me by my parents, teachers, pastors, professors, mentors, and kindred spirits guided me, gifted me into a life option that I could never have come up with on my own.

That life option was essentially a path called "self-give-away." It was the path of love.

Because of my Christian, Catholic faith and the hundreds of influences it had put in my path, I had come to embrace a vision, a journey, a set of commitments, a worldview that had steered my steps into some unlikely places, including, as I pondered death, the very unexpected place of gratitude instead of regret or resentment. I remember that I felt lucky to have spent almost all my adult life under the sway of a message that love in action, love given over—to friends, neighbors, family, strangers, the poor, the refugee, the sick, the vulnerable—could not only change a piece of the world but it would fill me up. I could die contented that I had lived life well—not perfectly, but with enough investment in love that it would carry me into death without fear or regret. I felt very lucky, fortunate, and even blessed as I prepared for the prospect of dying.

Well, it didn't happen. Despite having to stop chemo after one treatment because of the side effects, I made some lifestyle changes, and without knowing for sure what worked or what happened, I survived. Fourteen years later, no cancer. Again, I felt/ feel grateful.

Like most people who experience a brush with death, the experience was a gift. It reinforced the spiritual insight that all of life is a gift, that every moment matters, that our decisions and choices matter, that how we spend our time matters, that everything and everyone is precious.

The experience only reinforced for me the primary insight of our faith: God is love. The rest is commentary.

Every one of us—Catholic or not, Christian or not, religious or not—will necessarily, knowingly or unknowingly, invest ourselves into some life narrative that names what is worth living for. Some of us will choose to pursue wealth, some will choose mountain climbing, some will pursue power and fame, some will choose privacy. There are a thousand narratives to choose from, each competing with the others for our attention. The words of this book are essentially one narrative about how to best spend the one precious life that each of us has. I happen to be convinced that it is the most compelling narrative, the one most likely to fill us up.

So, in conclusion, here is the invitation one more time in short form: The Gospel invites us to love big, so love your kids, your parents, your soulmates, and your neighbors. Love your mail carrier, your work colleagues, and the strangers you pass by each day. And love the unemployed, the medically uninsured, the kids in dangerous neighborhoods, the homeless. Love the stranger, the refugee, the person with a different skin color or religion or political opinion. Love the vulnerable, the abandoned, and the war-torn. Love them all. Give yourself over to that love. God is on your side.

And do all this love together. Do this with a people in a place where love is celebrated, preached, proclaimed, commissioned, and encouraged. Like a parish. Doing this together makes it better, more powerful, more joyful.

Let us love the world together. Now. Before we die. It will be good and possibly great.

Appendix

A Five-Year Plan for a Vatican II, Mission-Oriented Parish

In their groundbreaking document *Communities of Salt and Light: Reflections on the Social Mission of the Parish,* the US Catholic bishops issued a call in 1993 for the growth and integration of social mission in the DNA of parish life. They wrote,

> In these challenging days, we believe that the Catholic community needs to be more than ever a source of clear moral vision and effective action. We are called to be the "salt of the earth" and "light of the world" in the words of the Scriptures (cf. Mt 5:13–16). This task belongs to every believer and every parish. It cannot be assigned to a few or simply delegated to diocesan or national structures. The pursuit of justice and peace is an essential part of what makes a parish Catholic.

They go on to speak to a vision of the integration of social mission into the life of the parish, including religious education, worship, preaching, and leadership. Their stated hope is that social mission will become a more robust part of parish life.

This appendix was originally offered as a resource through JustFaith Ministries; revised and expanded with permission.

Over the years of traveling to parishes, one of the most repeated requests I receive is for a resource that speaks to the *practical* steps of starting and growing a social ministry. This is understandable given that social ministry is a relatively new focus in parish life. In addition, there are very few books written on the subject and very few priests and lay leaders who have much experience in the area.

So, what follows is an attempt to provide one way to think about starting and expanding a social ministry. It is an amalgam of best practices I have been a part of or seen across the country along with a dose of my own imagination.

It is not intended to be understood as the only way to approach social ministry or even the best way to approach the task of developing social ministry; rather, it is meant to communicate possibilities. It is a way of describing the possible scope of what social ministry evolution and maturation might look like. Each of the five "phases" includes five suggestions.

For the purposes of communicating how this five-phase plan might be mapped out on a calendar, consider the possibility of thinking of it as five-year plan. In other words, this is not a small task that can be begun and finished in short order. Nor is it appropriate to think of it as a literal five-year plan because some things will be accomplished more slowly or quickly, depending upon the parish and how deliberate or aggressive it is about making progress. Moreover, it is likely that some parishes will find that they are already doing parts of some of the phases; hence, adaptation is the operative word.

This blueprint is only worthwhile to the extent that it prompts and encourages your own work in your own parish. So, again, let this material serve your imagination, creativity, and local reality.

Phase One (Year One)—Getting Started

Phase One presumes that a parish is just getting started. Furthermore, in what follows, it is assumed that a small group of parishioners—instead of, for example, the pastor or a parish staff person—is the instrument for first introducing a social ministry focus to the parish. Adapt these steps to your own situation as needed and as appropriate. Also, please realize that the five items described in this first phase are not meant in any way to be an exhaustive description of what should happen during this phase, but they do provide some important steps.

1. Preplanning

Let us imagine that there are five or six parishioners who have had some occasion to recognize their common interest in developing a social ministry in their local parish. The prompt might be a gathering where they meet and share common backgrounds and interests, or it might be a JustFaith Ministries program experience, or a Catholic Campaign for Human Development (CCHD) Journey to Justice Retreat. In any event, I have in mind that they all attend the same parish and it is a parish that does not currently include a structured or developed approach to the work of social ministry, that is, it is a parish where there is no standing committee that focuses on social ministry and where there is little evidence of social ministry activity.

The first step for this small group is simply to gather and discuss possibilities. We will call this group the Exploratory Group. It is recommended that this small group of people begin their first meeting by sharing prayer and telling their stories, including how they came to be interested in social ministry. In addition, consider the following three activities before proceeding to step #2 of Phase One. This will probably mean that the Exploratory Group will meet several times before moving to step #2. Do not rush these steps.

The first (and highly recommended) activity for the Exploratory Group is to obtain copies of *Communities of Salt and Light* to read and discuss together. This is an important step, as it will provide a framework for the work that lies ahead. It also will serve to define the essential parameters of social ministry, making clear that social ministry cannot be a single-focus, single-issue effort involving pet projects. In fact, many social ministry efforts suffer from the very outset by difficult and dead-end conversations about "the most important issue."

The second activity is to contact diocesan staff who are involved in working with parishes and ask for advice about how to proceed with this task. The staff might be found in a diocesan office titled Life, Justice and Peace / Respect Life and Social Justice / Office of Social Concerns, etc. If no such staff exists in your diocese or area, you might consider inviting someone with a long and respected history of involvement; quite often, there are women religious who have been engaged in significant ways who would be delighted to support these beginning efforts.

The third activity is to connect with social ministry committees of parishes that have a reputation of active social ministry work. If possible, meet with them (even by phone if necessary) to discuss best ways to approach the task of getting started.

2. *Approaching the Pastor*

Parishes are led by priests; a pastor's support of a project is critical. When the Exploratory Group has completed the tasks offered in step #1, they should ask the pastor for an opportunity to meet with him concerning the possibility of creating a social ministry to be overseen by a "social concerns coordinating team." To this end, it would be helpful to provide the priest with a copy of *Communities of Salt and Light* prior to meeting with him.

When you meet, thoroughly explain to him the steps you have taken thus far in preparation for your meeting with him. Allow an opportunity for each person present at the meeting to share their own faith experience leading to the conviction of the importance of social mission. Ask your pastor to share any experiences he has had.

It is likely that your pastor will already have a very full schedule; thus, it is important to explain that you are not asking him to *do* the work or to be engaged more than he would choose to be. Be clear that you want him to feel confident about what you are doing and that you are committed to regular communication with him, should he approve of the group proceeding.

During the meeting with the pastor, be sure to clarify expectations: What steps would come next? What else might he need from you before he could approve any next steps? How would ongoing communication happen? How would accountability to or representation on the parish council happen?

3. *Creating a Social Concerns Coordinating Team*

After getting approval from the pastor, it is recommended that the Exploratory Group begin the task of pulling together a formal parish committee. One proven strategy is to recruit for a team of ten to twelve. To that end, the Exploratory Group should consider how many of its own members will become part of the Social Concerns Coordinating Team and determine how many more people need to be invited to the team. Then the group should get a copy of the parish directory and make a list of those parishioners who seem to have both the interest and skills to be on such a team. If other people in the parish are already involved in some version of social ministry, give them strong consideration. This list should be prioritized and people contacted personally. Starting at the top of the list, potential candidates should be called to set up an appointment to *talk in person*. It's very important that this recruitment be done in person, so that a thorough explanation can be provided and invitation warmly extended. There is no recruiting strategy that has a better track record of success.

Continue meeting and inviting until the target number of ten to twelve people agree to make at least a one-year commitment to be on the team and attend monthly meetings on a specified day and time of the month (for example, the second Tuesday of the month from 7:00 p.m. to 8:30 p.m.).

Having ten to twelve people at a meeting provides the critical energy and breadth of experience. It is often the case that church committees will put a note in the parish bulletin asking for volunteers and proceed with whomever and whatever number responds. This is *not* an effective way to build the coordinating team. Rather, spend the time needed to meet with, talk to, and formally (and intentionally) recruit ten or twelve people. Consider parishioners who are not already involved but are regular members, and pay attention to diversity of age, gender, income, ethnic group, and so on.

Once—and not until—you have ten to twelve people committed, someone in the Exploratory Group should presume to organize and chair the first meeting. This will mean identifying the location, informing the pastor, and assigning responsibilities for refreshments, prayer, and note-taking. At this first meeting, be sure to allow ample time for prayer and plenty of time for people to introduce themselves. Remember, this is a community of faith not only committed to God's call for justice but to relationship with each other.

The work of the first meeting might also include a brief overview of the Exploratory Group's work followed by an overview of the *Communities of Salt and Light* document. Be sure to have enough copies of the document for each person, and ask all members to read the document carefully before next month's meeting if they are not already familiar with it. Also at this first meeting, be sure to elect or appoint a chairperson (or co-chairpersons).

One approach that the team might consider is that each of the seven elements of the *Communities of Salt and Light* document be attended to by at least one of the members of the newly formed Social Concerns Coordinating Team. That would mean, for example, members of the team who are particularly interested in liturgy would become the team watchdog for opportunities to link the work of the committee with the liturgical life of the parish. Other elements of *Communities of Salt and Light* would be similarly represented and attended to by one or more of the team members. Obviously, the team's work is not to do everything that comes to mind, but to discern and prioritize the options that come to light.

Each monthly meeting of the Social Concerns Coordinating Team should include the following: prayer, an educational component (speaker, video, or discussion of an article), consideration of the seven elements of *Communities of Salt and Light*, and some time for socializing and refreshments. Other items that might be included in the meetings are review of old or unfinished business, new projects/proposals for the team to consider, a brainstorming session for new ideas.

Within the first six months of the team's forming, it is highly recommended that there be an opportunity for the team to participate in an overnight retreat to build relationships, share life stories, and consider their work together. Such experiences go a long way in building team cohesion, understanding of one another, the faith life of the group, and commitment.

4. *Starting Subcommittees*

Later in the first year, the Social Concerns Coordinating Team will want to begin to establish subcommittees. These are working groups of people who all are committed to some specific or focused dimension of the work of social ministry. These subgroups could be expansions of a focus of one of the seven elements of *Communities of Salt and Light,* or could be inspired by a focus such as homelessness, or could be prompted by an organizational commitment to the local Catholic Charities, Pax Christi, St. Vincent de Paul, or Habitat for Humanity. Subcommittees should be initiated in response to notable interest among parishioners; remember, the focus of the team and the subcommittees is to organize the work and engage the parish, not promote pet projects or personal agendas.

In this first phase of a five-phase process, it is probably prudent not to attempt to initiate more than one or two subcommittees due to the work involved. That is, the process of starting subcommittees reiterates the process of starting the Social Concerns Coordinating Team itself. This includes identifying and recruiting ten or so additional people for the subcommittee, people who will commit to meeting monthly for at least a year.

All subcommittees should meet monthly (on a day different from the Social Concerns Coordinating Team). In addition, it is critical that all subcommittees be represented by one person at the Social Concerns Coordinating Team monthly meetings.

5. *Planning for Phase Two or Year Two*

It is important for any parish group to think strategically and intentionally about what it hopes to accomplish in the coming year. Engaging the team and each subcommittee in a process that looks ahead to defining the goals for the next year is a helpful exercise. Realize that a strategic plan is not meant to be an impediment to spontaneity or a rigid definition of what the team or subcommittee can or can't do. Rather, the process of planning prompts creativity, defines hopes, recommends practical steps and describes how social action will happen. This kind of planning should take place every year.

It also is important to keep the pastor informed and to integrate the Social Concerns Coordinating Team planning with the parish planning and budgeting process. It would also be appropriate to communicate with the pastor and the parish council about the possibility of establishing a budget for social ministry. Many dioceses have staff members who are skilled in strategic planning and can assist groups with this step.

Phase Two represents some of the possible results of a strategic planning process in Phase One.

Phase Two (Year Two)—
Continuation of Early Development

It should be noted that many of the suggestions in Phase One can and should be repeated in later phases. For example, there could/should be a social justice retreat planned every year, and there should be regular social concerns learning opportunities planned in the parish for, well, the rest of eternity!

1. Initiating JustFaith

The historical record clearly documents that the JustFaith program (see Chapter 9) builds a constituency for social ministry. If JustFaith is to be pursued, the Social Concerns Coordinating Team will want to be very deliberate about recruiting participants and selecting co-facilitators for the JustFaith process. Contact the JustFaith Ministries Office (www.justfaith.org) for more information.

One important agenda item for the team to take very seriously is how to integrate the JustFaith graduates into the work of social ministry in the parish. Graduates are typically eager to get involved soon after the program is over; it is important that they are provided options inside the parish and/or with organizations and agencies in the community.

2. *Starting Two More Subcommittees*

The development of the parish's social mission needs to engage more and more parishioners in an ever-broadening range of social ministry opportunities. As you expand the number of subcommittees, focus on the elements of *Communities of Salt and Light* or *Two Feet of Love in Action* (another document of the United States Conference of Catholic Bishops [USCCB]). These subcommittees might be formed around an area of interest (like racism or hunger), an organization (like St. Vincent de Paul or Habitat for Humanity), or the formation of a Global Solidarity Committee (through Catholic Relief Services [CRS]).

The creation and definition of a subcommittee allows for building important relationships in the community, as someone in the parish serves as a liaison between the parish/subcommittee and the organization. Critical opportunities for love in action can be recognized, communicated, and extended through the subcommittee to the larger parish.

Again, remember that every subcommittee must send a representative to the monthly meetings of the Social Concerns Coordinating Team. In fact, such representatives become part of the defined composition of the team. In other words, as social ministry matures and evolves, the team becomes a body of representatives of the various subcommittees as they come to be formed. This is critically important for the purposes of communication, calendaring, and mutual support.

Finally, as subcommittees mature, it is appropriate to ask members to make a two-year commitment instead of a one-year commitment. A minimum two-year term allows for the development of some expertise and assures more continuity. I also recommend that after a maximum of three two-year terms (a total of six years), members be required to take at least a one-year break before being invited back to the committee. Term limits allow people to take a well-deserved sabbatical and encourage new membership and fresh thinking.

3. *Offering a Social Justice Retreat*

It is important to engage the parish in opportunities to understand the profoundly intimate relationship between prayer and action. Offering retreats is a good way to accomplish this. The team may want to initiate a yearly retreat during a specified month that allows twenty-five to seventy-five people to spend a weekend exploring the spiritual dimensions of social ministry. It is an oft-neglected area that partly accounts for social ministry's underdevelopment. It is worthwhile to spend the time necessary to identify retreat directors who have this kind of expertise.

4. *Planning Regular Educational Opportunities for the Parish*

If regular educational events have not already been part of the activity of the parish, Phase Two is a good time to start. The Social Concerns Coordinating Team or an appropriate subcommittee (for example, a Social Concerns Formation and Education subcommittee) will want to coordinate a regular opportunity for the larger parish to be introduced to some component of social ministry: an organization, Scripture and theology, Catholic social teaching, a current issue, and so forth. When feasible and appropriate, such sessions can and should be integrated into the larger formation schedule of the parish. On the other hand, it is also appropriate to schedule such opportunities at special times or even create a regular time that such opportunities occur. These educational opportunities should occur on a regular basis. I might also recommend the use of JustFaith Ministries' *JustMatters* modules for ongoing educational opportunities (see www.justfaith.org).

5. *Connecting with Local and National Organizations*

As the team and subcommittees develop and mature, you will want to be linked with as many effective local and national social ministry organizations as feasible. Some national organizations include the Catholic Campaign for Human Development (CCHD), Catholic Relief Services (CRS), Catholic Charities USA and the local Catholic Charities agency, Bread for the World, Maryknoll, Pax Christi, St. Vincent de Paul, the Center of Concern, and the USCCB Office of Justice, Peace, and Human Development, to name a few.

It is important that the team discern both the needs of the parish and the local community *and* which organizational links are most critical to the growth of social ministry now in the life of the parish. Prioritizing is a critical element in your planning; you simply can't do everything.

Phase 3 (Year 3)—Expanding Horizons

1. Continuing JustFaith

Although it takes some planning and energy to continue to offer JustFaith in the parish year after year, the testimonies of parishes that have made such a commitment attest to the significant benefits of doing so. To be able to anticipate that each year eight to fifteen new JustFaith graduates will be ready to make significant commitments to the work of social ministry is like having a social ministry catechumenate! It is appropriate at this stage to create a JustFaith Subcommittee (or separate task force) that is dedicated to supporting JustFaith by promoting the program, recruiting participants, assisting co-facilitators, and mentoring participants as/ when needed.

2. Starting Two More Subcommittees

(See #2 in Phase Two for the logic of expanding the number of subcommittees.) The selection about what subcommittees to start can be a product of many kinds of influences, including parishioner interest, local needs, some kind of crisis, or a factor of what kinds of projects or emphases the team takes on. So, as mentioned above, the team may opt to start a JustFaith Subcommittee or task force, if it feels this is necessary or helpful to sustain the process. Or the team may opt to start an Advocacy Subcommittee to support and sustain legislative priorities of the diocese and the Church (see below). Again, the choices about what kinds of subcommittees to start and how many to start will vary significantly from parish to parish even within the same city or diocese. What is important is that the Social Concerns Coordinating Team makes it a priority to expand the number of subcommittees.

3. Beginning Sister Parish/Twinning Relationships

One of the most potent ways to engage parishioners in the work of social mission is to provide opportunities for them to link in direct relationship with brothers and sisters in other places, especially those communities experiencing crisis; this speaks to Pope Francis's emphasis on *encuentro* (encounter). Sister parishes or twinning relationships afford an occasion for parishioners to encounter the human face of oppression, hunger, violence, deprivation, or poverty. These kinds of relationships can be formed locally, nationally, or internationally. For example, a middle-class or wealthy parish might offer to twin with the nearest rural parish that is serving a newly settled population of migrant families. Such twinning allows for potlucks, prayer together, storytelling, and ultimately the opportunity to care for and about each other.

In addition, twinning relationships with parishes in poor countries can be powerfully impactful; however, the cost of travel and the time involved typically prohibits many parishioners from participating. One solution is to start two twinning relationships—one local and one international. A Twinning Subcommittee might be created to oversee these activities.

Another way to enter into sister parish or twinning relationships is by first starting a subcommittee or a parish Global Solidarity Committee. Contact Catholic Relief Services (CRS) for assistance with starting this committee.

4. Encouraging Legislative Advocacy

Engaging parishioners in the political side of a faith-based justice ministry is important and called for by the Catholic bishops of the United States. This work also is widely avoided and often misunderstood. The Social Concerns Coordinating Team will want to spend some time and energy concentrating its attention on this very important dimension of social ministry work. This would include presentations and homilies on the Catholic social teaching about civic responsibility and participation as well as the broader vision of our faith tradition. It also would include bringing in speakers from the state Catholic Conference and Bread for the World, doing workshops on how to write effective letters and approach legislators in their offices, offering field trips to lobby at the state capital, and so on. Other helpful resources for legislative advocacy can be found through the Office of Justice, Peace, and Human Development at the USCCB and through Catholic Charities USA.

This is work that generates enthusiasm especially when done with larger groups. It is exciting and effective to have fifty or a hundred parishioners take fifteen minutes after liturgy to write letters to their legislators while they share a cup of coffee.

5. *Quarterly Celebrations*

As the work of social ministry diversifies and expands, it is very important to remember that it is still largely countercultural, that it meets with much resistance from many places, and that it engages people of faith in an open-sightedness that gives view to an enormous amount of human suffering. This is difficult work. The inspiration of God's Spirit is that it brings people of faith— brings the Church—together.

To this end, it is important to provide an opportunity for all those who are involved in social ministry—and any other parishioners who would like to attend—to gather periodically in a large group. These gatherings should be engaging, light on agenda, and a time for joyful celebration. Encourage everyone involved in any dimension of social ministry work to come to an evening potluck dinner that includes time to socialize, a thoughtfully planned prayer service, opportunities to share social ministry success stories, and perhaps a short educational presentation on the Good News of God's call to compassion.

These kinds of gatherings are important because they are celebrations of a common call and a common mission. They should be pleasant, happy, and fun. By gathering everyone together, it bolsters commitment by allowing everyone to see the breadth of commitment in the parish.

Phase 4 (Year 4)—Advanced Work

1. *Offering JustFaith, Engaging Spirituality, and/or Good News People*

Offering these three JustFaith Ministries programs helps with the ongoing formation of parishioners and the preparation of leaders for the work of social ministry. In parishes where social ministry is alive and growing, parishioners become increasingly aware of the Christian call to be a vessel of God's healing presence in the world. For many, this awareness awakens an appetite for formational experiences, such as those offered by JustFaith Ministries. There are very few organizations dedicated to the formation for social ministry; JustFaith Ministries has a long and well-recognized reputation in parishes all over the country. Over sixty thousand people have participated, and many of them are now the social ministry leaders in their diocese or parish.

2. *Linking with Projects Receiving CCHD Funding*

If your parish is located in an area where there is a project or organization receiving CCHD (Catholic Campaign for Human Development) funding, build a relationship with this group. Working side by side with low-income people can be a powerful and successful strategy of social change. Most CCHD-funded projects invite participation with and collaboration by parishes that are both poor and nonpoor. Engaging your parish in this work is very important and potentially transformative for the parish at large.

3. *Starting Two More Subcommittees*

As stated repeatedly before, expanding subcommittee work is critical. Perhaps a subcommittee focused on CCHD or community organizing would be most appropriate considering #2 above.

4. *Organizing a Tithing Process for the Parish*

The tradition of tithing suggests that a portion (a tenth?) of what we are blessed with should be rerouted to those in greatest need as an expression of our commitment to God. This is true for each one of us, *and* it is especially true for churches of middle-income and upper-income households. There are many examples of parishes across the country that give a full 10 percent of the parish collection to local, national, and international causes that address the needs of our most desperate sisters and brothers.

The Social Concerns Coordinating Team may want to discuss with the pastor the possibility of presenting such a proposal to the parish council and the larger parish as an item to be discerned, discussed, and considered.

While there might be resistance to this idea initially, don't be discouraged. A discussion about tithing engages the larger parish in decision making about the proper use of the parish income, wealth, and resources. Such a commitment to share resources, should it be approved, brings added energy and wealth of many kinds to the parish. My personal experience of working at a parish in Louisville, Kentucky, that tithed was that it was a commitment that made parishioners proud of their community. There were some lean budget years during which some members and even the pastor suggested that we cut or eliminate the parish tithe; so strong was the commitment to the tithe that it was never reduced.

A special Tithing Subcommittee can be given responsibility for communicating the availability of such money to local organizations and for making decisions about the distribution of such funds based upon pastor-approved criteria.

5. *Exploring a Parish Social Ministry Position*

As the work of social ministry continues to expand, it will become clear that the parish would benefit from a full-time staff position to orchestrate and attend to this important ministry. As stated in the document *Communities of Salt and Light*, "Effective social ministry helps the parish not only do more, but be more—more of a reflection of the gospel, more of a worshipping and evangelizing people, more of a faithful community. It is an essential part of parish life."

A staff position in social ministry is evidence of the parish's full commitment to being a community of salt and light. A parish budget, much like the federal budget, is a kind of autobiography of the parish's values. To invest resources into a position that serves the parish's commitment to the poor, vulnerable, and wounded is a sign of a parish's determination to serve God, to serve the poor, and to involve itself in the invitation and mission of Jesus. In chapter 3, I propose as part of parish renewal that there ought to be as many positions committed to outreach as there are committed to education, administration, and worship. However, change can be slow. Starting with one position might be more workable in many places.

Phase 5 (Year 5)—Uncharted Creativity

1. *Inaugurating Multiyear Mission Trips*

As parishes take themselves seriously as communities of compassion and justice (communities of salt and light), they may well choose to consider and adapt the great witness of the communities of women and men religious who have committed themselves to the poor. In this regard, parishes may begin to make connections with places in this country or other countries in which there is great need and that would benefit from some expression of full-time service. The parish, in effect, becomes a place that inspires and prepares missionaries of care and solidarity. Such commitments could be one or more years in duration.

The parish may choose, for example, to engage with Maryknoll Lay Missioners, support the Global Fellows program of Catholic Relief Services, or come up with immersion and service options via its relationship with sister parishes. The Social Concerns Coordinating Team would promote and recruit those people who might be interested in making a one- to three-year commitment to serve in a place of need.

Some may think such options are beyond the reach of parishioners' commitment but remember, all those who joined Maryknoll or the Franciscans or the Jesuits as sisters, brothers, or priests started as parishioners!

The goal here is to provide options to parishioners who are ready to make a big commitment to an adventure of faith. A parish that allows for the possibility that some of its members will be interested in these kinds of invitations is a parish that honors the Spirit of God to inspire and empower. (See chapter 4 for more reflection on this option.)

2. *Starting a Catholic Worker Community*

Akin to #1 above, because it offers a rather challenging (and, as far as I know, untried) option, urban or suburban parishes may want to consider starting a Catholic Worker Community in the inner city to provide hospitality to those who are homeless. Historically, the witness of the Catholic Worker has been understood to be outside of the usual parameters of parish life, but that need not be. A parish or a cluster of parishes could commit themselves to the start-up and maintenance of a Catholic Worker house and provide opportunities for people to join an intentional community and commit to a remarkable social ministry. This would be an utterly new model of support and collaboration and allow for an extraordinary kind of solidarity between the parish and those who experience poverty. (See chapter 4.)

Like #1 above, this act would build a bridge between an extraordinary expression of Catholic witness and the local parish.

3. *Opening a Local Fair-Trade Store*

Part of the tradition of Catholic social teaching tries to engage the economic life of a community with the needs of the poor. That can be expressed in many, many ways. One way includes the opening of stores that market goods made by peoples in poverty-stricken places, people who need opportunities to sell their goods for fair and just compensation. Parishes may want to consider engaging themselves in the start-up and oversight of a store that markets fair-trade items.

Such a store would not only provide a wonderful alternative in the marketplace, but it could become a place of justice education about economic alternatives. Moreover, it could provide jobs for parishioners and/or unemployed neighbors.

4. *Developing Emergency Assistance Teams*

Hurricanes, floods, tornadoes, earthquakes, and other disasters happen. While organizations like the Red Cross and Catholic Charities can provide tremendous resources, it is true that what also is needed is a human presence or a willingness to help person to person. Parishes may want to invite and train a team of parishioners who want to and can serve in emergencies and do so with little notice. These might be people who not only have a desire to help in a time of crisis but also have some flexibility with their jobs and families. Preparing a team for such a situation allows for a quick and helpful response.

5. *Annual Social Concerns Award and Celebration*

As parish social ministry grows and matures, it is important to highlight and celebrate this work. One way to do this is to recognize and honor all those members of the parish who have made significant contributions to the work and whose lives are an inspiration to the parish. Hosting a yearly Social Concerns Awards Banquet provides an occasion for parishioners to gather, celebrate, and reflect on the social mission of the church. Honoring people in this way affirms the work, recognizes faithful responses to be salt and light, and highlights to the larger parish that this is what all are called to become.

Resources

United States Conference of Catholic Bishops. *Communities of Salt and Light: Reflections on the Social Mission of the Parish*, www.usccb.org.

———. *Two Feet of Love in Action*, www.usccb.org.

Acknowledgments

A lot of people have helped make this book possible. I thank my professors at Furman and Notre Dame who introduced me to the richness of theology and the transformative possibilities of the gospel; forty years later, I continue to draw from their teaching as I try to make sense of the sacred and holy in this wounded world.

I remember fondly the Bijou Community in Colorado Springs, where the fifteen of us spent our time befriending, feeding, and housing our sisters and brothers on the street, resisting violence, and trying to live a loving and simple life; it was the perfect learning adventure post-academia and the best possible place to meet my spouse.

I thank Fr. Joe Graffis, the pastor at Church of the Epiphany, who hired me as a member of the parish staff, for his support and his passion for justice and solidarity; with his encouragement, Just-Faith was born, and many, many lives were subsequently changed.

I thank Tom Ulrich, Kristi Schulenberg, and Mary Wright, who, as staff members of Catholic Charities USA and Catholic Campaign for Human Development, helped birth JustFaith as a national program; their frequent laughter reminded me that the obligation to serve, as hard as it can be sometimes, should include a sense of humor.

I thank my talented staff colleagues at JustFaith Ministries, especially Chris Breu, and so many remarkable board members, particularly Gary and Mary Becker, who all together formed the biggest social ministry test lab in the country; it was a distinctive gift to work with a staff who prayed and supped together every day and to work with a board with so little ego and such generosity.

I thank St. William Church, my parish, which is a lively, happy, holy version of Christian community. I am humbled by the goodness that gathers there every Sunday.

I thank Pope Francis for affirming that I have not been crazy the last thirty years, that social mission can and should be at the center of parish life.

I thank Robert Ellsberg, publisher of Orbis Books, for pestering me for a decade to write something, anything (please!).

Finally, I thank my gracious wife, Maggie, who has forgiven my many blindnesses and inspired me with her own simple, everyday acts of love to so many. I cannot imagine my life without her life.

Index

activities
  distraction of, 110
  in the logic model, 101, 102
  in parishes (logic model),
    106, 108, 110–16
affluence, exploitation and, 88
Archdiocese of Louisville,
  122
assets, in the logic model,
  100–101

Baltimore Catechism, 2–3, 121
baptism, ministry rooted in,
  4, 10
baptismal faith, 4, 10
Barber, Michael, 137
Benedict XVI, 9
Benedictines, 28
Benedict of Nursia, 92
Berry, Wendell, 88
Bethany, anointing at, 35,
  37–39

Bible, revolutionary themes
  of, 68
Boyle, Greg, 13, 28, 40, 41,
  47, 85
Bread for the World, xi, 75, 77,
  127, 154, 157
Brueggemann, Walter, ix
Burghardt, Walter, ix

calling, 137–38
Catholic Campaign for
  Human Development,
  xi, 28, 52, 77–78, 97,
  125, 127, 145, 154,
  158–59
Catholic Charities USA, xi,
  14, 28, 29, 52, 71, 97,
  126, 127, 150, 154, 157,
  163
Catholic Church
  community tradition of, 93
  future of, in the US, vii